Dear

I hope you find these
stories interesting. I promise
that none of these ghouls
and monsters can hurt you

They'll be frightened of
you!

lots of love

from

Liz xxx

✳ The Mystery and Magic Series ✳

Ghouls
and
Monsters

Robert Ingpen & Molly Perham

DRAGON'S WORLD

CHILDREN'S BOOKS

Dragon's World Ltd
Limpsfield
Surrey RH8 0DY
Great Britain

First published by Dragon's World Ltd, 1995

Editor: Diana Briscoe
Designer: Megra Mitchell
Design Assistants:
Karen Ferguson
Victoria Furbisher
Art Director: John Strange
Editorial Director: Pippa Rubinstein

British Library Cataloguing in Publication Data
The catalogue record for this book is available from the British Library.

ISBN 1 85028 299 4

Typeset by Dragon's World Ltd in Caslon, Century Old Style and Helvetica.
Printed in Italy

✳ Contents ✳

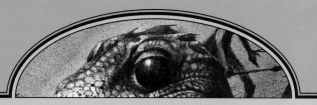

✳ Introduction ✳

Monsters, ghouls, evil spirits and strange beasts that are half-human, half-animal, appear in folklore around the world. These fearsome creatures threaten humans with their cruelty and wickedness, and traditional legends tell how brave men and women have outwitted or conquered them. Some monsters, such as the basilisk orthe sphynx, have characteristics of different animals, but have human wisdom and faculties. Others, like Medusa the gorgon, are humans that have been turned into beasts. In more recent years monsters have been created in scientific laboratories. These man-made monsters are just as frightening as the old dragons and giants.

In some parts of the world, demons and spirits exist in many different forms and with varying characteristics. Some are weak and appear only as whispering voices or as vague shadows, but many are powerful and evil creatures that cause trouble to humankind.

From earliest times people have believed that the dead can return from the grave to visit their loved ones. Certainly an evil criminal or someone who has been the victim of such a one, can return after death as a ghost. These tormented souls can haunt the world of the living until someone helps them to find peace.

Molly Perham

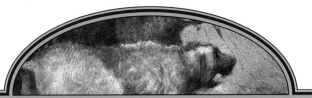

Monstrous Animals

Strange beasts, monsters and creatures that are half-human, half-animal have been reported in many parts of the world. Some of these mythical beings, such as the basilisk, the griffin and the sphinx, have features of different animals, combined with human wisdom and faculties. Others, like the werewolf and Medusa the gorgon, are humans that have been turned into beasts.

Monsters have immense strength and unnatural proportions. They threaten humans with their cruelty and wickedness, and legends tell how heroes have outwitted or conquered them.

WEREWOLF

In many countries there is a belief that people sometimes change into large and fierce animals such as wolves, tigers or bears. This belief may have come about because some hunting peoples disguise themselves in animal skins in order to get near their prey. The 'leopard men' of West Africa were said to dress themselves in leopard skins in order to kill and eat people. In another part of Africa a hunter once shot a hyena wearing gold earrings.

Werepeople turn into beasts at night and revert to human form at sunrise. In India a were-tigress was once caught in a trap, and next day the villagers found that the trap contained a naked woman. Another time a hunter may shoot at a wild animal during the night, and in the morning one of the villagers is seen limping with a wound in the leg.

In Europe, the animal that a person changes into is usually a wolf. 'Were' is an old name for man, so 'werewolf' means man-wolf. Transformation into a werewolf is often a form of punishment. But sometimes a person actually wants to become a werewolf in order to do evil or to take revenge on an enemy. The change from human being to wolf is brought about by performing various rituals. The right moment to make the change is at midnight, by the light of a full moon. The would-be werewolf draws a magic circle and builds a fire over which he places a cauldron containing a potion of herbs and drugs. Then he smears his body with an ointment made from the fat of a newly-killed cat, mixed with ingredients like aniseed and opium, and ties a wolfskin round his waist. Kneeling inside the circle as the magic potion simmers, he chants an incantation.

If the ritual has been properly carried out, the human body will gradually take on the characteristics of a wolf. Once fully transformed, the werewolf will be able to indulge in the traditional night-time activities of hunting, killing and eating. A woman who is changed into a werewolf eats her own and other women's children.

A true werewolf undergoes a complete transformation and looks just like a wolf. However, some manage to disguise the fact that they are wolves by wearing their fur on the inside. So anybody with small pointed ears, prominent teeth, strong curved fingernails, bushy eyebrows that meet over the nose, a third finger as long as the second on each hand, or even a lot of hair, should be regarded with suspicion.

A werewolf that is wounded or killed immediately becomes human again. The most effective way of doing this is to shoot the beast with a silver bullet.

▽ Prince Vseslav lived in Polotsk, now Belarus, in the 11th century. He was born with a caul on his head, at a time when there was an eclipse of the sun. These two accidents of birth gave him the magical powers of second sight and metamorphosis. Each night the prince turned into a wolf and rampaged around the countryside.

BASILISK

The basilisk, sometimes known as a cockatrice, is the king of the serpents. It is said to be produced when the egg of a cock is hatched by a serpent. It is about the size of a cat, with the body of a cock and the head and tail of a serpent. The crest, or comb, on its head is like a royal crown. There are two species of this fearsome monster. One is a kind of wandering Medusa's head – one glance from it causes instant horror followed by immediate death. The other species burns up whatever it is looking at. Birds fall from the sky, animals drop dead where they stand, while plants and shrubs wither and die.

All other serpents and snakes flee the moment they hear the distant hiss of their king. The only creatures that can stand up to the basilisk are the weasel and the cockerel. The weasel fights back with its sharp teeth, and knows that rue leaves will cure any wounds. At the sound of the cock's crow, the basilisk dies.

GORGON

In the legends of ancient Greece, the gorgons were monsters of the underworld. They were hideous winged creatures, with hissing snakes protruding from their large heads instead of hair. Their noses were flat, and their tongues lolled out over big teeth. Anyone who looked at a gorgon's horrible face was turned to stone.

The gorgons were the three daughters of the sea god Phorcys and his wife Ceto, and were called Stheno the mighty, Euryale the far-leaping, and Medusa the Queen. Medusa was the only one who was mortal. She had once been a lovely maiden whose hair was her chief glory. Medusa dared to compare her beauty with that of Athene, and in a fit of rage the goddess turned the lovely hair into hissing serpents.

One of the Greek myths tells how Perseus conquered Medusa and cut off her head. Perseus was the son of Zeus and Danae. When he was born his grandfather, King Acrisius of Argos, consulted an oracle and was told that the child would one day slay him. Acrisius was so horrified when he heard this that he shut his daughter and her infant son up in a chest and set them adrift on the sea. They were rescued by Polydectes.

When Perseus had grown to manhood, Polydectes told him about the monster Medusa, and asked him to set out and conquer her. The gods came to his aid, giving him winged shoes to fly with, a sword and a shield, and the Cap of Darkness which made him invisible.

Medusa lived in a foul, dank cavern, and as Perseus approached he saw that all around lay the stony figures of men and animals that had caught a glimpse of her and been petrified at the sight. Wearing the Cap of Darkness Perseus was able to approach unseen. He held the shield in front of his eyes to avoid looking at the monster, and guided himself by the reflections. Closer and closer he crept until he was able to reach out and strike off Medusa's head.

Now that Perseus had Medusa's head he possessed a powerful weapon. With its help he rescued a maiden called Andromeda from a sea monster, by turning it to stone. When Perseus reached home he found that Polydectes was persecuting his mother, and was able to destroy him, too.

Eventually Perseus returned to Argos and by accident killed King Acrisius with a discus which he threw during some games. And so the prophecy was fulfilled.

PHOENIX

The ancient Greeks told stories about a strange bird called a phoenix. It was about the size and shape of an eagle, and very brightly-coloured.

According to legend, there is only one phoenix at a time.

▽ The Phoenicians probably named their country after the magnificent phoenix. Its colouring suggests that it must be a member of the peacock family.

It usually lives in Arabia, though it has also been seen in Egypt. The phoenix lives for 500 years, then it makes a nest of spices and lays one egg. When the heat of the sun sets the nest on fire, it is burned to a cinder. After a few days another phoenix hatches from the ashes.

GRIFFIN

The griffin is a monster with the head and wings of an eagle, the body of a lion, and the pointed ears of a dog. Its talons are so large that the people of Turkey and Iraq, where the griffin lives, make them into drinking cups.

A griffin is the offspring of a lion and an eagle, but it is eight times larger than a lion and stronger than a hundred eagles. Like the eagle it builds a nest, but instead of an egg, it lays an agate.

Griffins know by instinct where buried treasure lies, and they watch over gold mines and punish humans who try to steal from them. Many

▷ Griffins vary in colour from a rather drab, tawny yellow to pure white, golden, or cream flecked with scarlet. Their wing feathers may range from dull brown to bright blue and green.

a thief has been torn apart by the claws of a griffin that was patrolling the skies.

However one race of people, the one-eyed Arimaspians, managed to get the better of the griffins. Near where they lived there was a desert full of gold-dust, which the griffins guarded. The Arimaspians used to steal the gold-dust at the hottest time of day, when the griffins were underground sheltering from the sun. Then they rode away on she-camels that moved very swiftly because they were anxious to get back to their young foals at home.

The griffins' other task is to draw the chariots of the gods. They regard horses as competitors for this task, and therefore prey on them. A griffin is strong enough to carry off a full-sized horse.

The griffin is also known as a gryphon.

Sphinx

The sphinx was a female monster, with a lion's body, the wings of an eagle and the face and breasts of a woman. According to Greek legend, the goddess Hera sent a sphinx to the city of Thebes to punish the people for their drunkenness, after Dionysus had taught them how to make wine. The sphinx lay crouched on the top of a rock and accosted all travellers who went past and asked them a riddle. Those who solved it were allowed to pass safely by, but those who failed were killed and eaten.

No one succeeded in solving the riddle and at last the ruler Creon proclaimed that he would give his kingdom to the first person who guessed it.

About then, Oedipus's journeys led him to Thebes. When Oedipus was a baby an oracle had predicted that he would kill his father and marry his mother. He was in self-imposed exile, but had already unwittingly killed his father, Laius.

The sphinx pounced on Oedipus and asked her riddle, 'What animal is that which in the morning goes on four legs, at noon on two, and in the evening upon three?'

Oedipus replied, 'Why man, of course. As a baby he crawls on all fours; later he walks on two legs, and in old age he needs the support of a stick.'

The sphinx was so angry that someone had managed to solve her riddle, she threw herself off the rock and was killed.

As for Oedipus, he became king of Thebes and married the queen, Jocasta – thus fulfilling the second part of the prophecy that he would become the husband of his own mother.

Prince Ivan and the Golden Bird

Many years ago, in Russia, a Tsar had a magnificent garden where all the trees had gold and silver leaves, and bore precious stones as fruit.

The Tsar's favourite tree grew apples of pure gold, with pearls inside instead of pips. However, every night a bird with golden plumage came flying into the garden and plucked a few of the apples, so that soon there were hardly any left. So the Tsar summoned his three sons and said, 'Whichever one of you catches the golden bird will have half my kingdom, and after my death he will receive it all.'

That night Dmitri, the eldest son, sat down under the tree and waited for the bird to appear. But he grew tired and fell asleep, and the golden bird took some apples and flew away again. The following night Vassily, the second son, went to watch in the garden. He, too, fell fast asleep and did not hear the bird when it came and picked the apples.

The third night Ivan, the youngest son, took his turn. He had been watching for several hours when suddenly the whole garden began to glow, as if hundreds of candles were burning. The golden bird was sitting on the tree plucking the apples. Ivan caught hold of the bird's long tail, but it tore itself free and rose into the sky, leaving behind one golden feather. This shone so brightly that it lit up the whole palace.

The golden bird did not come into the garden again, but the Tsar wanted more than anything to own it. So the brothers set out in quest for it, and each rode off in different directions.

Ivan eventually came to a signpost with this message written on it:

HE WHO RIDES STRAIGHT ON, WILL BE COLD AND HUNGRY.
HE WHO RIDES TO THE LEFT WILL BE WELL HIMSELF, BUT HIS HORSE WILL DIE.
HE WHO CHOOSES THE RIGHT-HAND PATH WILL BE KILLED,
BUT HIS HORSE WILL REMAIN ALIVE.

Ivan chose the left-hand path, and soon met a huge grey wolf that set upon and killed his horse. But then the wolf offered to carry Ivan on its back instead, and towards nightfall they came to a high stone wall.

'Climb over the wall into the garden,' said the wolf. 'You will find the golden bird in a golden cage. Take the bird, but do not take the cage.'

Ivan could not resist the beautiful cage, but as soon as he touched it there was a great clanging of an alarm. The watchman woke and caught him. When the owner heard that Ivan was the Tsar's son he said, 'If you had asked me properly I would have given you the bird. But I will forgive you if you get me Tsar Affron's horse with the golden mane.'

Ivan sat on the wolf's back again and towards nightfall they came to the white stone walls of Tsar Affron's stables.

'Go into the stables and fetch the golden-maned steed,' said the wolf, 'but do not take the golden bridle that hangs next to it.'

Ivan could not resist the beautiful bridle, but as soon as he tried to take it off the hook there was a noise like thunder. Armed guards came running from all directions, and took Ivan before the Tsar. When Tsar Affron heard who Ivan was, he said, 'Go and get me the Tsarina Helena the Beautiful, whom I love with all my heart. Then I will give you the horse and bridle.'

When they came to the golden railing round the Tsarina's garden the wolf said, 'Go back up the road and wait for me under that great oak tree.'

The wolf snatched the Tsarina when she came out for her evening walk, and flung her on his back. When Ivan saw them coming along the road he too jumped on. But as they approached Tsar Affron's palace Ivan became very sad because he had fallen in love with the Tsarina himself.

'Don't be sad,' said the wolf, 'I will change myself into Helena the Beautiful and you can take me to the Tsar in exchange for the golden-maned horse.'

Tsar Affron was delighted to receive his bride. Ivan mounted the steed and galloped away, carrying the real Helena with him. About ten minutes later, the grey wolf caught them up.

However Ivan was reluctant to give up the wonderful horse in return for the golden cage, so he asked the grey wolf to play the same trick again.

So that was how Prince Ivan rode home on a golden-maned steed with the beautiful Tsarina, carrying the golden bird in its golden cage.

KELPIE

The kelpie is a water spirit that haunts Scottish rivers and lochs in the shape of a horse. He lures people to mount on his back, and then plunges them into deep water, where he devours them, all except the liver which floats to shore.

▷ When the kelpie appears in equine form, it is as a splendid young horse wearing a magic bridle. Anyone who takes off the bridle and replaces it with an ordinary one can make the kelpie work for them. However, the owner should beware of making the kelpie work too hard, or it will curse its owner and his children.

One story tells of seven little girls who were out walking one Sunday when they saw a pretty little horse grazing near the loch. One after another they got on its back, which gradually lengthened so that there was room for them all to sit. A boy who was with them saw this happening, and refused to join them. The horse turned its head and yelled, 'Come on, scabby-head, get up too!' The boy ran for his life, and the kelpie with the seven little girls plunged into the loch. Only their entrails came back to land.

A kelpie will also show himself as a rough, shaggy man. In this shape, he will leap up behind a solitary rider, gripping and crushing him, and frightening him to death.

On another occasion a kelpie took on the appearance of a handsome young man. But the girl he was courting discovered his true identity by the shells and weeds she found in his hair when she combed it for him. Then he turned into a horse and pursued her home.

Before storms, kelpies can be heard howling and wailing, and you can sometimes see their hooves galloping across the surface of the water. The only way to subdue a kelpie is to put a bridle on him.

SALAMANDER

The salamander in myth is a small black and yellow lizard that likes to live in very hot temperatures. Its preferred habitat is the slopes of volcanoes, and it especially enjoys it when an eruption of red-hot lava pours down the slopes. However, occasionally one will agree to live in a fireplace.

Alchemists used salamanders as temperature gauges when they were turning lead into gold. When the fire was hot enough to begin the conversion process, the salamander would leap into the blazing coals.

MANTICORE

This fearsome monster is said to live in the forests of Indonesia, Malaysia, and India. It has the body of a lion and the head of an ugly old man with a huge mouth full of teeth. Its tail is scaly like a snake, and at the tip there is a ball of poison darts.

The manticore stalks hunters through the tropical forests and once it has cornered a victim, it fires a volley of poisonous darts at him. Every morsel of flesh and bone of the victim is scrunched up by the razor-sharp teeth.

RATWIFE

Few animals are more disliked by human beings than rats. Brown rats came from Norway aboard Viking longships and soon colonized the whole world. They are able to live in all climates, and in cold places grow long coats to keep themselves warm. Rats like to live wherever there are people, travelling through the sewers and up into the basements of houses and barns.

Once you have rats in your home, it is very difficult to get rid of the cunning creatures. In Norway rats are kept under control by ratwives. If a town is invaded by these creatures the town councillors will call in a ratwife and negotiate a fee for their removal.

The ratwife knows that rats, like humans, are fond of music. She will go and stand in the town square after nightfall, and the moment the moon is up, she begins to play slow, caressing notes on her pipe. Gradually her tune becomes more and more lively and urgent, and then so sonorous and piercing that it penetrates into the furthest alleys and cellars of the town.

Soon, from the depths of the cellars to the top of the attics, out come the rats. They pour onto the streets and head towards the town hall, so squeezed together that they look like the waves of a flooding torrent. When the square is full the ratwife leads the rats away, playing continuously on her pipe, to the nearest stretch of water. In Norway no town is very far away from a river, a lake, or a fjord.

When she reaches water, the ratwife climbs into a boat and pulls away from the shore. The rats, still mesmerized by the music, plunge in after her and drown.

YETI

▽ The yeti is almost certainly related to Bigfoot, although the two creatures live in very different parts of the world.

Reports of shaggy wild men go back for centuries. Folklore is full of stories of huge hairy giants and shambling, man-like brutes who have an appetite for human flesh. The most famous is the yeti, or Abominable Snowman, of the Himalayas. The local people, the Sherpas, who are best placed to know, firmly believe in it and are afraid of it. They say that there is also a female of the species, with breasts so large she has to throw them over her shoulder before she bends down.

One of the first reports of a giant hairy creature looking somewhat like an earlier form of human came in the early part of the nineteenth century. An erect, tailless being with shaggy black hair ambled up to some local people and they fled in terror. They called the creature a raksha, the Sanskrit word for 'demon'. Rakshas have appeared in Indian literature for over four thousand years.

Giant footprints in the snows of Mount Everest were discovered by British mountaineers in 1953, and these are the most tangible evidence of the yeti so far.

BIGFOOT

In the remote mountains and forests of western Canada and the northwestern United States there have been hundreds of sightings of an apeman known as Bigfoot, or by the Indian name of sasquatch. He is said to be very tall, and covered with reddish-brown hair. His forehead slopes backwards, and he has little or no neck.

The Native Americans have told stories about Bigfoot for centuries, but the first recorded sighting by a European occurred in 1811. An explorer who was crossing the Rockies in an attempt to reach the Columbia River came across a huge set of footprints with only four toes.

Since then more and more giant wild men of the woods have been seen and written about, and it became clear to the experts that these creatures were more violent and dangerous than their kin, the yeti. This was confirmed in 1910 when two prospectors were found in the Nahanni Valley in the northwest territories of Canada with their heads cut off. The sasquatches who had been seen in the area were blamed for the murder, and from then on it became known locally as Headless Valley.

BARBEGAZI

The mountainous regions of Switzerland and France are inhabited by gnome-like people called barbegazi. They live in caves and tunnels high up in the topmost peaks, and are rarely seen by humans because they never venture down below the tree-line. The barbegazi are said to whistle or hoot to warn mountaineers of an impending avalanche. Certainly they only appear when the temperature is really freezing and blizzards force mountaineers down from the highest altitudes.

The barbegazi look like gnomes from other regions, except that their hair and beards are covered in icicles. The name 'barbegazi' comes from the French words for frozen beards – *barbes glacées*. These little people wear white fur garments that make them invisible against the snow. Their large feet act as snowshoes, enabling them to travel across the slopes with remarkable speed.

Very few humans have ever seen a barbegazi, but it is thought that they help St Bernard dogs to rescue people trapped in the snow. On a couple of occasions a barbegazi has been caught and taken down to the village, but the gnomes cannot survive when the temperature rises above zero.

▽ Unlike other snow creatures, the barbegazi gnomes hibernate during the warmer months and emerge only after the first heavy snowfall.

St George and the Dragon

Heroic battles against monsters occur frequently in legends from all parts of the world. St George was a Christian soldier who was martyred at Lydda in Palestine in about AD 300. His fame rests on the popular medieval tale of how he rescued a princess from a terrible dragon.

Silene, a city of Lybia, was troubled by a dragon that had taken up residence in a lake just outside the walls and was terrorizing the neighbourhood all around. The king had sent armed forces to deal with the monster, but its breath poisoned anyone who approached.

At first the unhappy citizens had managed to stay the dragon's appetite by giving it two sheep every day. But after a few months their flocks were exhausted and it was agreed that one person should be chosen daily by lot and sacrificed to save the others.

Eventually the lot fell on the king's daughter, and though her father offered all his treasure to spare her, the citizens insisted that she must suffer with the rest. Eight days' grace was the sole concession made to her youth and royal blood. At the end of that time she was led to the lakeside.

George came along at that moment and found the tearful princess waiting for the dragon to come for his breakfast. She begged him to save himself while there was still time, but the brave knight refused to leave. He went down on his knees, prayed to God for help, and then prepared to defend her.

The dragon soon appeared and George mounted his charger. Together they attacked the dragon in a fierce charge. George pierced the dragon's thick hide with his lance, but did not kill it. When it rolled on its back in surrender, the princess tied her girdle round its neck, and led the defeated monster back to Silene in triumph.

George explained to the delighted people of Silene that he had only conquered with Christ's help. When the king and his people promised to become Christians, St George cut off the dragon's head.

KING KONG

T he increasing number of reports that giant creatures may exist in remote parts of the world has provided the inspiration for several monster films.

In *King Kong*, a film-maker called Carl Denham discovers a lost land of dinosaurs and pteradactyls on Skull Island, ruled over by Kong, a giant ape. The monster is captured and taken back to New York, but he breaks loose and wrecks Manhattan. Eventually he climbs to the top of the Empire State Building and is shot down by fighter planes.

In another film, a mad scientist tries to control the giant apes with a remote-control device. The ultimate King Kong movie is the one in which the giant ape battles against a fifty-foot tall Japanese monster called Godzilla on top of Mount Fuji.

GODZILLA

Godzilla is a giant green dinosaur (based on a *Tyrannosaurus rex*) which has radioactive breath. He lives on Monster Island with all the other Earth monsters. He has starred in nearly thirty films, mostly made in Japan.

As well as his meeting with King Kong (see opposite), Godzilla has battled against many other kinds of creatures during his film career. These have included huge caterpillars, a robot duplicate of himself, a metallic insect called Megalon, and a smog monster created from the sludge and industrial pollution in Japan.

In *Godzilla vs Gigan* the antagonists are enormous cockroaches. The story opens as a Japanese comic book writer called Ishikawa takes a job at a new amusement park called Children's Land, designing monsters for rides in the Godzilla Tower. He and his friends discover that things are not quite as they appear to be.

Children's Land is in fact being built by aliens from another planet and the amusement park is a cover for their real project, world conquest. The aliens, though they look like humans, are actually big cockroaches in disguise. They bring the space monsters Ghidrah and Gigan with them to conquer Earth.

After Ishikawa warns the beasts on Monster Island, a fierce battle takes place between the space monsters and the Earth monsters Godzilla and Anguirus, which the Earth monsters eventually win.

Monsters of Europe

Tales of heroes and giants, monsters and maidens, evil spirits and wicked goblins abound in European folklore. Monstrous creatures are symbolic of the eternal struggle between good and evil. They represent the force of evil and are usually overcome or outwitted by a much smaller hero.

Grendel and his Mother

Beowulf is one of the oldest poems in the English language – the only manuscript can be seen in the British Library in London. It tells of a brave young hero who defeated evil in the form of a malevolent water monster called Grendel.

In the far-off days when Hrothgar was King of Denmark, a dreadful monster called Grendel terrorized the countryside. Every night Grendel came out of the lonely marshes nearby and burst into the gold-roofed hall called Heorot where the king's warriors were sleeping. Seizing one of Hrothgar's men in his huge arms, Grendel carried him back to his lair deep in the marshes, and devoured him. This continued for twelve years, until the great hall was left derelict and deserted.

News of this reign of terror spread far and wide. Eventually Beowulf, who was the nephew of the King of the Geats of Sweden, heard of Hrothgar's misery and sailed to Denmark with fourteen companions. Hrothgar welcomed Beowulf joyfully, but feared that even he would not be able to defeat Grendel. That evening the warriors feasted and drank together, but when night fell they began to fear Grendel's coming.

Beowulf kept watch while his companions slept, and it wasn't long before he heard the monster crashing through the great barred doors of the hall. With one swift movement Grendel snatched up one of the sleeping men, tore him apart, and devoured the flesh in great gulps. Then he turned in Beowulf's direction and lunged at him. But Beowulf was faster than the monster. He grasped one of the huge arms with his bare hands and after a furious struggle wrenched it from its socket. Howling and bleeding, Grendel returned to the marshes to die.

Next day Hrothgar and his nobles returned to Heorot, and people came from far and wide to rejoice at their delivery from the terrible monster. That night, however, Grendel's mother, an even more fearsome creature, came to the hall seeking revenge and carried off the king's chief counsellor.

Beowulf chased after her, armed with his magic sword Hrunting, and followed her down to her lair at the bottom of a muddy lake. Grendel's mother attacked Beowulf savagely and came close to killing him, but in the end he managed to slay her with his sword.

As Beowulf was about to leave he saw Grendel's corpse lying in a corner of the lair. Cutting off the head, he carried it back to Heorot in triumph.

BANSHEE

Some Irish families have a guardian spirit called a banshee who watches over them. She is generally supposed to be the spirit of a beautiful maiden of the family who died before her time, but she usually appears as an old woman with straggly black hair and eyes red from weeping. When any member of the family is about to die the banshee utters a mournful keening or screaming in the night. If several banshees are seen together it means that there will be a terrible accident.

The word banshee is an old Irish name for 'woman of the fairies'. People are rather proud of having an ancestral banshee in the family, for it shows that they belong to one of the old families of Ireland. The banshee will even travel abroad with her family, if they emigrate to another country.

There is also a Highland banshee who devotes herself to a particular Scottish clan. She is seen by a burn or loch, washing the clothes of those who are about to die in battle.

OLD LADY OF THE ELDER TREES

Elder trees traditionally have magical powers. The flowers, berries and even the wood itself are ingredients for potions used in both black and white magic. The stake that is driven through a vampire's heart should always be made from an elder tree, but it is very unlucky to

use the wood for making furniture or other household items. A baby placed in a cradle made from elder wood will never thrive, and if you build a house with it, the timbers will warp and rot.

According to an old legend, the magical powers of the elder are controlled by the Old Lady of the Elder Trees, whose spirit lives inside each tree. She comes from Denmark, the original home of elder trees, but her descendants

have emigrated to most parts of Europe. In Germany, men doff their hats whenever they pass an elder tree in recognition of her presence.

The Old Lady of the Elder Trees has white hair the same colour as the elder flowers, and she wears a dress as black as the berries. She hobbles about with a stick made from elder wood, and is rarely seen.

However, if you want to use wood from the elder tree there is a way to neutralize the Old Lady's unfriendly powers. When you are cutting it, you should say the following words: 'Old Lady of the Elder Tree, please give me some of your wood, and when I grow into a tree you may have some of mine.'

BLACK ANNIS

People in Leicestershire have traditionally had small windows in their houses so that Black Annis can get no more than her arm inside. Black Annis is a horrible old hag with a blue face and iron claws who lives in the Dane Hills of Leicestershire. Her home is a cave, called Black Annis Bower Close, which she dug out of the rock with her own nails. The old hag hides in a great oak tree at the entrance to the cave, then leaps out to catch unsuspecting children.

Black Annis only goes out when it is dark. When people hear her grinding her long teeth they bolt their doors and keep well away from the windows.

▽ Black Annis has also been seen in the Scottish Highlands, where she sits outside a cave on a pile of bones. No one is quite sure if these are the bones of sheep and deer, or whether they are human remains.

Giants

Giants are popular characters in European myths and legends. In some places they were revered as gods; in others they were monsters who represented a great force of evil, and more often than not were overcome by a much smaller hero, representing the force of good.

Giants vary greatly in size and type, from Gogmagog, who was a mere ten feet high, to the giant Bolster, who had a stride of six miles. A few were gentle and well-disposed to men, but most were rapacious and destructive and caused trouble by gobbling up flocks of sheep, drinking rivers dry, trampling crops underfoot or tearing mountains apart.

In Greek myths there are earth-born giants (or Titans) who leap mountains to reach the sky and do battle against the gods. One of the mighty deeds of Hercules was his fight against the Titans. In Scandinavian legends there are frost giants who constantly try to outwit the Norse gods.

The ancient Britons worshipped giants as gods. They cut huge outlines of them on the turf of hill slopes, and you can still see these near the villages of Cerne Abbas and Wilmington. They thought that Stonehenge and clusters of rock in Cornwall that look like castles were built by giants. After the giants were forgotten as gods, all sorts of stories grew up about them. King Arthur's knights are said to have fought giants such as Tarquin of Manchester and Carados of Shrewsbury.

Legendary giants are often those responsible for some topographical detail of the landscape, such as a hill, mound or rock. Sometimes rocks or land formations are supposed to be petrified giants, or objects dropped by giants. The Giant's Causeway on the coast of Northern Ireland was said to be the beginning of a road from Ireland to Staffa made by a giant.

Most giants were male, but several of them had wives as large and powerful as themselves. The Giant Wade and his wife Bell built the Roman road that is called Wade's Wife's Causeway. Wade did the paving and Bell carried the stones in her apron. Once or twice her apron strings gave way, leaving a large heap of stones on that spot.

GOGMAGOG

It is said that in ancient times Britain, then called Albion, was ruled by a race of giants. Their number was gradually diminishing as they fought and destroyed each other.

When Brutus was exiled from Troy for accidentally killing his father, he and another Trojan called Corineus sailed to Albion and landed at Totnes in Devon.

Brutus killed most of the giants and divided the land among his followers. Corineus got the part that we now call Cornwall, and it was

there that the largest and most powerful giant still lurked.

When Gogmagog heard that Corineus had taken over his territory he rallied the remaining giants and pounded across the countryside to attack. But Corineus managed to dodge his whirling club and struck off Gogmagog's head. The giant's huge body was thrown over a cliff, which to this day is still called the Giant's Leap.

GREEN MAN

This evil spirit of the English countryside flits through the trees waiting for a chance to pounce on wood cutters and gamekeepers. When he blunders through the woods it sounds as if leaves are rustling or branches breaking, or a storm is blowing through the treetops.

The Green Man's colour is a good camouflage, though no one is sure whether he is a naked man with green flesh or if he is made of green wood, with leafy branches for arms. He is sometimes a character that comes with Morris dancers; then he looks like a cone of leaves.

WILL O' THE WISP

The nebulous flickering lights that you sometimes see at night over marshy ground are those of Will o' the Wisp. The light resembles a flame and appears fixed in position, shining steadily close to the ground. It is often mistaken for the light of a lantern, but any foolish traveller who follows such a light will find that it retreats as he advances, and very soon he will fall into a swamp or pond and drown.

Will o' the Wisp's real name is

Ignis Fatuus, which means 'the foolish fire', and in different parts of England he is known by a variety of other names. In Shropshire, there was a Will the Smith who was so wicked that he was barred from Hell as well as Heaven. He was given a piece of burning coal to warm himself, and condemned to flicker over boggy ground, where he lured travellers to their death.

In West Yorkshire this spirit is called Billy-w'-t'-wisp; in central England his name is Hobbledy's lantern, Hobby-lantern or Jack-a-Lantern; in the southwest he is Joan-in-the-Wad or Kitty Candlestick. To these may be added Friar Rush (see ABBEY LUBBER), Gyl Burnt-Tayle, Hinky Punk, Spunkies, Puck and Robin Goodfellow, all of whom amused themselves with Will o' the Wisp pranks.

There are various accounts of Will o' the Wisp's origins. Some think he is a ghost, who cannot rest because he committed a sin before his death. A man who moved his neighbour's boundary stones was thought to be doomed to haunt the area with a flickering light.

ABBEY LUBBER

In the days when there were abbeys all over Europe, devils called Abbey Lubbers used to tempt the monks to have feasts and enjoy themselves instead of praying and doing good works. One famous Abbey Lubber was called Friar Rush. He led the monks into all kinds of evil ways before he was eventually discovered. Friar Rush was banished from the monastery and became a Will o' the Wisp. The monks were so shocked by what had happened that they led virtuous lives for ever afterwards.

REDCAP

According to old English and Scottish legends, a Redcap is an evil goblin who preys on travellers and dyes his cap in their spilled blood. The red cap distinguishes him from ordinary goblins. A Redcap has long grey hair and a beard and looks like an ugly, little old man. His other distinguishing features are fiery red eyes, vicious eagle's claws instead of hands and heavy iron boots.

Redcaps live in ruined castles and watchtowers along the border between Scotland and England. If you get caught by one the only way you can escape is to quote a few words from the Bible, or show him a cross, and then he will give a dismal yell and immediately disappear.

◁ One of the Scots lairds is said to have kept a Redcap as a familiar, rather as a witch keeps a cat. He was a particularly cruel and wicked man, and was hated by the villagers who lived on his estate. The Redcap prevented any weapons from causing harm to his master, but in the end the villagers destroyed the evil laird by boiling him in oil.

Trolls

Trolls are the giants of the Scandinavian wilderness. They are said to live in caves in the mountains, guarding heaps of gold and silver. By day they stride off into the dark forests, returning home at nightfall to feast and sleep. The sight of the sun is fatal to trolls: one glimpse of the sun's glory and they either burst or turn to stone.

In Finland there was once a troll who lived on a mountainside overlooking a bay. On the opposite side of the bay lived a farmer with three sons.

One day he said to them, 'We work hard like honest Finns and remain as poor as church mice, while that wicked old troll grows richer and richer. I think it's time for you boys to take his riches from him and drive him away.' The youngest son, whose name was Olli, agreed at once. So the two elder boys, shamed by his boldness, had no choice but to go with him.

The troll greeted them cordially. 'You are the sons of the Finn who lives across the bay, aren't you?' he said. 'I am glad to see you because my daughters need husbands. Marry them and you will inherit my riches.'

The brothers were delighted to agree to this, and after a good supper the troll sent them all to bed.

But first he gave the youths red nightcaps and his daughters white ones. The older brothers suspected nothing and soon fell asleep. Olli waited until everything was quiet and then he changed the caps so that the girls wore the red ones.

Presently the old troll came over to the beds with a long knife and with three swift blows cut off the heads under the red caps. As soon as Olli heard the troll snoring he roused his brothers and they hurried home across the bay.

Before long Olli announced that he was going back to the troll's cave again. The farmer tried to dissuade him, but Olli only laughed.

'I've heard that he has a horse with hairs of gold and silver,' he said. 'When you see me again, I'll be riding that horse.'

The troll wasn't at home, but his wife was there. She asked Olli to take the horse and water it while he was waiting. But instead of leading it to the lake, Olli jumped on its back and galloped off to the other side of the bay.

Olli's brothers were envious of the horse with gold and silver hairs, and warned him sourly, 'You'd better be careful, or the old troll will get you!'

A few days later Olli announced, 'I think I'll go over and get the troll's money bags.'

Again he found the troll's wife alone. She wanted to keep Olli there until the troll came home, so she pretended that she was tired and asked him to

watch the bread in the oven while she rested on the bed. But before she knew it, she had fallen asleep. Olli reached under the bed, pulled out their money bags full of gold and silver pieces, and hurried home.

A few days later Olli said, 'Do you know, the troll has a beautiful coverlet woven of silk and gold. I think I'll go over and get it.' He took with him a drill and a can of water, and when it was dark climbed on top of the cave and bored a hole right over the bed. As soon as the troll and his wife were asleep he sprinkled some water on the coverlet and on their faces.

The troll woke with a start. 'I'm wet,' he said, 'the roof must be leaking.'

The wife threw the wet coverlet over a line to dry, and when they were asleep again Olli made the hole a little bigger and reached in to get the coverlet. Then he ran off back home.

A few days later Olli said, 'There's still one thing in the troll's cave that I think I ought to get. It's a golden bell. If I get that bell then there will be nothing left that would be better owned by an honest Finn.'

So he went again to the cave and waited until the troll and his wife were asleep. As he reached out to grab the bell it tinkled and woke the troll.

'Ha! Ha!' he cried. 'I've got you now and this time you won't get away.'

The troll told his wife to heat up the oven ready to roast Olli while he went off to invite all the trolls who lived on the other side of the mountain to a lavish feast.

When the oven was ready the troll's wife said to Olli, 'Now then, my boy, sit down in front of the oven with your back to the opening and then I'll push you in.'

Olli pretended he didn't understand. He sat down first one way and then

another until the wife got impatient and showed him how to do it.
With one shove Olli pushed her inside the oven and slammed
the door. Then he took the golden bell and went home.

In due course the troll and his guests came trooping in
and sat down to supper. As the troll was slicing the
roasted flesh his knife struck something hard.
Looking down he saw that it was a bead from the
necklace that his wife always wore.

Next day at dawn the troll went down to the
shore and hollered across the water.

'Olli?' he called. 'Have you got my golden
bell? And did you roast my old woman?'

'Yes, I've got your golden bell,' Olli
replied. 'But as for your old woman –
look, is that her?' He pointed at the
rising sun which was coming up
behind the troll.

The troll turned and
looked. He looked
straight at the sun,
and then he burst.
And that was
the end of the
wicked troll.

Monsters of the Americas

The Americas were once inhabited by a large number of different tribes, each with its own culture. Among them were the buffalo hunters of the Great Plains, the fishermen of the northwestern coast, the seed-gatherers of the western desert, the corn planters of the east, the tropical forest peoples of the West Indies and the Incas and other peoples who lived in the Andes.

Each tribal culture had its own myths and legends to explain the world they lived in and the forces that governed their lives.

The Great Bear Chief

In the forests of the Northwest, a man lived in a small hut with his wife, three sons and a little daughter. At the end of a hard winter food was scarce. One morning the three boys set off to hunt, looking for animal tracks in the snow.

The boys kept together for some time, until they reached a place where the path divided. The youngest brother went to the right, while the others took the trail to the left. They had not gone far when their dogs scented a bear and drove it out of the undergrowth. The elder boy shot it right through the head.

When the boys reached home their father said, 'What, only one bear? When I was a young man we used to get two bears in one day.'

The boys were disappointed to hear this, and next morning they set off again, following the same trail as before. As they reached the fork a bear ran out from behind a tree and took the trail on the right. The two elder boys pursued him and the second son, who was also a good shot, killed it with an arrow. On the way back they met up with the youngest brother, who had also shot a bear himself.

The boys threw the two bears triumphantly on to the floor of the hut, but their father said, 'When I was a young man, I used to get three bears in one day.'

So the next day the brothers brought back three bears; and the day after that four bears.

Every time a bear was killed its shadow returned to the great bear chief, who lived far away in a high mountain. He was furious that so many bears were being shot.

On the fifth day the youngest boy stayed at home. A rise in the temperature had made the snow soft and slushy, and the bow strings of the elder boys hung loose. A bear rushed out of the undergrowth and, without stopping to think that their bows were useless, they chased after it.

The bear led the boys right into the mountain,

where they found themselves surrounded on all sides by a council of bears.

'Why are you killing all my servants?' asked the great bear chief. 'Look at their shadows, with your arrows sticking in them. Now you will not hurt my people any more, because you will become bears yourselves.'

The bear chief dipped a handful of moss in some spring water and rubbed it on their arms and legs, which changed into those of a bear. And so they would have to go on all fours for the rest of their lives.

When the two boys did not return home, their father set out to look for them. But the great bear chief had prepared a trap and he fell headlong into it and broke his neck. Then the mother put on her snowshoes and went out into the forest, and she too fell into the pit beside her husband.

Finally the youngest boy said to his little sister, 'All the food has gone. I will have to go out and hunt for some more, otherwise we will both starve to death.'

He made himself a new bow and cut some arrows, then called his dog, Redmouth, and set out along the same trail as before.

The bear chief, knowing that the boy would eventually come along, had sent a bear to wait in the bushes. But he hadn't reckoned on Redmouth,

who barked loudly and frightened the bear, and then chased after him. The boy followed, but got left behind, so that by the time he reached the mountain both of the animals had vanished, but he could hear Redmouth barking inside.

'Let my dog out at once, bear chief!' he yelled. 'Otherwise I will destroy your mountain.'

The bear chief laughed, which made the boy so angry that he aimed one of his arrows at the bottom of the mountain and shot straight through it.

As the arrow touched the ground there was a great rumbling and the mountain burst into flames. The bear chief and his servants were all consumed in the fire, but when it had finally burnt itself out the boy found his two brothers alive. They stood up on their hind legs and stretched out their paws to beg him for help.

Seeing some moss growing by a spring nearby, the boy tore up a handful of it and rubbed it on his brothers' arms and legs. Immediately the bearskins fell off them and they stood upright once more.

So the three brothers hurried home to look after their little sister, who soon forgot that she had ever had a father and mother.

ACHERI

This skeletal, squaw-like creature is a female ghost of the Amerindian tribes. She sleeps during the day and appears at nightfall, wearing a tattered deerskin dress and carrying a small tom-tom. Her voice is as eerie as the wailing of wolves in winter, and anyone who hears her chant knows that death will soon come, either to them or to a member of their family.

The only way to protect yourself against the acheri's death chant is to wear red garments or beads. This colour will keep you quite safe. Anyone dressed completely in red need have no fear at all.

CHENOO

The Iroquois tribes of North America believed that in the early days there was a race of evil giants whose bodies were fashioned out of stone. These stone giants, or chenoos, decided to invade the Indian territory and exterminate the race of men. A party of Indians just starting on the warpath learned of the invasion, and were instructed by the gods to challenge the stone giants to combat.

This they did, and the two bands of opponents faced each other at a spot near a great gulf. But as the giants advanced on the Indians the god of the west wind, who was lying

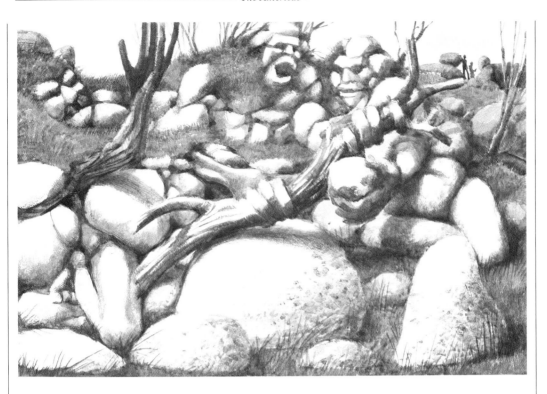

in wait for them, swooped down on the chenoos and hurled them over the edge of the gulf, far down into the abyss below. There they perished, and the stones of their bodies lie there still.

BOKWUS

T he bokwus lives in the forests of northwestern America. He is rarely seen by humans, but hunters often sense his presence in the densest parts of the forest and sometimes they catch a glimpse of him between the branches. His evil face is camouflaged with warpaint.

Fishermen in particular should watch out for the bokwus. It is difficult to hear him above the sound of running water. While a fisherman is busy with his catch, the bokwus creeps closer and closer until he can push him into the river. When the fisherman has drowned, the bokwus grabs his soul and takes it back to his forest home.

BAYKOK

T he baykok is a night spirit of the Chippewa Indians of North America. He looks like a walking skeleton, except that his bones are covered by a thin, translucent skin. His eye sockets glow in the dark with a dull red light that terrifies those who see it.

The spirit preys on warriors, who can sometimes hear him coming because his bones creak and rattle as he walks. However, there is no escape from the baykok. He kills by striking a warrior with his club, or by shooting invisible arrows.

AHUIZOTL

I t is rumoured that this fearsome monster lives at the bottom of a lake in Central America. The ahuizotl gets extremely angry when fishermen take fish from the lake, and has been known to create violent storms by lashing its huge tail from side to side. Any unfortunate fisherman who falls overboard is quickly eaten. Sometimes it is possible to deceive the ahuizotl by hiding some of the catch at the bottom of the boat and throwing the rest back into the water. The monster then thinks that the fisherman has not taken any of its property.

JOY BOY

T his West Indian spirit cures all the problems of mankind by tapping out an hypnotic rhythm on his drum. Whoever hears the music instantly forgets their troubles and is compelled to sing and dance until they drop from exhaustion.

EL NIÑO

T he Incas and other peoples of the Andes in South America believed in a cosmic power that had great influence. Some people think that the huge stone heads on Easter Island are a representation of it. The Spanish invaders called the cosmic power El Niño.

El Niño controls the climate of the southern Pacific, and is responsible for the winds and currents on which the fishermen's livelihood depends. When humans obey the fundamental laws of

nature, El Niño does everything possible to assist them. When they break the laws, there may well be disastrous results. For example, El Niño has caused climatic changes as a punishment for overfishing. And even as far away as Australia, a series of droughts has resulted from damaging the environment.

ZOMBIE

O f all the supernatural horrors that sorcery has in store for the unwary, becoming a zombie is the most dreaded fate of all. A zombie is a corpse that has been brought back to life by a voodoo priest, or houngan. Usually a zombie is created as an act of revenge, but sometimes zombies are made simply to provide cheap and uncomplaining labour.

Zombies only move around at night, and must return to their graves before sunrise. Anyone who sees one in the darkness might not necessarily realize it is a corpse. They move with a slow, shambling walk and their heads are always lowered so that they do not have to look anyone in the eye.

Once corpses become zombies they can never escape from their animated state unless they taste salt. They then become aware of their fate and, knowing they are dead, will return to the grave forever.

In Haiti elaborate precautions are taken to prevent houngans from raising the dead and creating zombies. Coffins are buried beneath solid concrete, or the graves are dug close to a busy road with plenty of passers-by. However, some years ago a zombie wandered back to his own village and eventually someone plucked up the courage to give him a drink of salt water. He then stammered out his name, and was identified as a man who had died and been buried four years before. A priest was called and the zombie revealed the name of a houngan for whom he and a band of other zombies had been forced to work.

People who have died in accidents become a different type of zombie. They rise from their graves and wander around harmlessly at night. Eventually, when they reach the end of their natural life span, they settle peacefully in their graves.

The Rest of the World

In Middle and Far Eastern countries, and in Africa, China, Japan and Oceania, gods, demons and spirits exist in many different forms and with varying characteristics. Some are weak and appear only as whispering voices or as vague shadows, but many are powerful and evil creatures that cause trouble to humankind.

Spirits inhabit mountains, lakes, rivers, seas, bogs and marshes. They lurk in the branches of trees, crevices of the earth, or come up from under ground. Natural phenomena like the wind, thunder and lighting, and the fire of volcanoes, are all said to be controlled by gods and spirits.

WIND GODS AND SPIRITS

Gods and spirits control the weather in all parts of the world. Sometimes they have a benign influence, helping to provide good harvests and fishing, and favourable winds for seafarers. At other times they are malevolent, like the genies of Arabia who stir up sandstorms in the desert.

In some countries, one principal god is in charge of the wind. Quetzalcoatl was the Aztec god of the wind, although he often delegated the task to lesser gods.

Ah-dad of ancient Babylon had two distinct sides to his personality: sometimes he rode on a charging bull carrying a thunderbolt in his hands; at other times he brought spring breezes and soft rain.

Often a single god is not sufficient to control all the winds. Four brothers – Boreas, Zephyrus, Eurus and Notus – are responsible for Mediterranean winds. A number of individual spirits are responsible for the different types of wind that affect Australia, but Bara, who brings the rain-bearing north wind, is important in northern areas.

There are several Japanese gods of wind and weather. Haya Ji, the god of the whirlwind (shown opposite), carries the wind in a leather sack and releases it as a punishment when human beings have violated the laws of nature.

Yama-uba

The yama-uba is a fearsome female spirit of Japan. Long ago an ox driver who was carrying a load of salted mackerel met a yama-uba high up in a mountain pass.

'Ox driver, give me a mackerel,' she called.

The ox driver reluctantly took a mackerel from his cart and threw it to the yama-uba. While she was eating it, he tried to hurry past. But the ox moved so slowly that they had only gone a few paces before the yama-uba was demanding another. One by one he threw all the mackerel to her until there were none left.

The yama-uba now demanded the ox, and threatened to eat the ox driver unless he gave it to her. Scared out of his wits, the poor man took to his heels, leaving the ox behind.

The yama-uba quickly crunched up the ox and then chased after the ox driver again.

'Now I am going to eat you!' she shouted.

The ox driver ran as fast as he could until he came to the shore of a lake. He climbed up a tree to hide, but his reflection showed in the water below.

When the yama-uba came panting after him she saw the reflection and thinking that the ox driver was in the lake, plunged in after him.

While she was floundering around the ox driver jumped down from the tree and started running again. At the foot of the mountain he came to a house and dashed inside. Unfortunately it happened to be the house of the yama-uba, and before long he heard her pounding and puffing up to the door. Quickly he climbed up into the rafters and hid himself.

The yama-uba followed him in and made up a fire

in the hearth to bake some rice cakes. She dozed off while waiting for them to cook, so the ox driver pulled a straw out of the thatched roof above him and, reaching down, picked up the rice cakes one at a time and ate them.

The yama-uba woke up and roared, 'Who has eaten my rice cakes?'

The ox driver said in a soft voice, 'Fire god! Fire god!'

Grumbling to herself, the yama-uba put a kettle on the fire to heat some wine, and again she dozed off.

Taking another straw from the thatch, the ox driver drank all the wine.

'Who has drunk my wine?' thundered the yama-uba when she awoke.

'Fire god! Fire god!' whispered the ox driver.

'Oh well, I might as well get some rest,' said the yama-uba, and climbed into a big wooden chest that she used as a bed.

As soon as he heard her snoring the ox driver climbed down from the rafters and drilled some holes in the lid of the chest.

Then he heated up some water until it was boiling and poured it through the holes. And so the ox driver got his revenge on the greedy yama-uba.

ONI

In Jigoku, the underground hell of Japan, there are evil spirits known as oni. These horrible creatures have red and green bodies, and the heads of

horses. They ride out in chariots of fire looking for dying sinnersand carry them back to Jigoku for judgement. The sinners stand before a truth-telling mirror: men are judged by Emma Hoo, the king of Jigoku, and women by his sister.

KAPPA

The kappa is a demon who is said to live in Japanese rivers. He lies in wait for people and animals who get too close to the water's edge and drags them under. Then he eats them from the inside out.

The kappa is a greenish-coloured dwarf with a shell like that of a tortoise on his back. On the crown of his head there is a circular depression which must be kept filled with water.

Anyone who meets a kappa should give him a polite bow. The kappa will then return the greeting, and the water will pour out of the depression in his head, leaving him completely powerless.

The Fisherman and the Afreet

A genie, or jinn, is a spirit that can take human or animal form. Genies have supernatural powers over human affairs, and may have a good or evil influence. In this tale from *The Arabian Nights*, an evil genie, called an afreet, is set free by an unsuspecting fisherman.

There once lived a fisherman who was very poor. Every morning he went out to catch fish, but would never throw his net into the sea more than four times. This was one of the rules of his life.

One morning just before dawn he threw out his net, and as he drew it in, it felt that it was much heavier than usual.

'I must have a fine catch this time,' he said to himself. But all that was in the net was the dead body of a donkey.

The fisherman cast a second time, and again found it hard to draw the net in. But there were no fish, only a basket of mud and sand. The third throw produced only stones and shells.

The day was now beginning to dawn, and the fisherman knelt down to say his prayers, as was his custom. 'O Lord, you know that I only throw my net into the sea four times a day. I have cast three times today without a catch. One more only remains. I beg you to be kind to me as you were to Moses.'

For the fourth time the net was thrown. Again there were no fish, only a copper bottle, which seemed to be full of something, for it was very heavy.

'I will sell this bottle in the market,' said the fisherman. 'I will get more for it than I would for a hundred fishes. But first I want to see what is inside.'

As he pulled out the stopper smoke poured from the bottle. After a little while it collected together and took the shape of a huge afreet. His head was up in the clouds, while his feet rested on the ground. The afreet was terrifying to look at. Inside his cavern-like mouth were teeth like stones. His nostrils were like trumpets; his eyes glowed like lamps.

The fisherman wanted to run away, but was so afraid that he could not lift a foot.

'Solomon, Prophet of God,' cried the afreet. 'I ask your pardon, and I will never go against your will again – I promise.'

On hearing this the fisherman became a little

bolder. 'What are you saying? The great King Solomon has been dead for nearly two thousand years.'

'I will tell you my story,' said the afreet, 'before I kill you.'

'Why do you want to kill me?' asked the fisherman. 'I have set you free. Are you going to return good with evil?'

'I have to kill you,' said the afreet. 'But as you are a good fisherman, I will grant you one favour.'

'What is that?'

'I will allow you to choose the manner of your death,' replied the afreet.

Then he added, 'King Solomon shut me up in this bottle to punish me. He gave orders to the jinn to throw the bottle into the sea. I vowed that the person who pulled me out in the first hundred years would become a very rich man. But time went by, and no one pulled me out. Two more centuries passed and I became so angry I vowed that I would kill the person who set me free, but would allow him to choose how he should die.'

'Take back your vow,' said the fisherman, 'and God will forgive you.'

'No,' said the afreet. 'I can't do that. You must die.'

The fisherman felt faint with terror, but he pulled himself together and said, 'Then I must submit to God's will. But first I must ask you something.'

'Be quick then,' said the afreet. 'What do you want to know?'

'I wish to know if you were really in that bottle. I find it difficult to believe. Do you swear it by the name of God?'

'I swear it,' said the afreet.

'Why,' said the fisherman, with a laugh, 'that bottle is not big enough to hold one of your feet, let alone your whole body.'

'I will show you,' said the afreet. He instantly turned back into smoke and curled into the bottle.

The fisherman quickly jammed the stopper back into the bottle and then threw the bottle back into the sea. Then he went home, praising Allah for his deliverance from the evil spirit.

RAKSHASHA

Rakshashas are the evil spirits of India. It is said that the god Brahma created the rakshashas out of his foot and made them guardians of the precious primal waters on earth.

There are several different types, ranging from the quite friendly, through those that wander about at night scaring people, the ghouls who haunt cemeteries and devour corpses, to the dangerous, powerful giants who have attacked the gods.

▷ The story of how Prince Rama fought Ravana, with the help of Hanuman the monkey-king, is told in the great Indian epic, the *Ramayana.* Ravana had kidnapped Rama's wife, Sita, and imprisoned her on a faraway island. After much searching, Rama and Hanuman found Sita and rescued her. Rama fought a duel with Ravana and defeated him with a poison dart.

Rakshashas have the heads of reptiles, donkeys, horses or ordinary human heads. They come in every conceivable shape and size, some being quite handsome while others are revoltingly ugly. Some have crooked legs, long protruding teeth and bulging eyes; others are as fat and heavy as elephants. Some are dwarfs and others are giants.

Female demons are called rakshashi, and they usually have drooping bellies and breasts. With their poisonous nails they kill and tear up human bodies, and devour the flesh.

The lord of all the rakshashas is named Ravana. He has ten heads and twenty arms which grow again as soon as they are cut off. He was defeated by Prince Rama in battle.

YAKKU

If someone becomes ill in India, people sometimes say that they have fallen prey to a yakku, a demon of disease. Yakkus live in inhospitable, dark places such as derelict buildings, overgrown gardens, caves or other crevices of the earth. They are all servants of the great devil of disease, Maha-Kola-Sanni-Yaksaya.

Each yakku is responsible for one particular type of disease and appears at an appointed hour of the day. When that hour comes, the yakku assumes a disguise and may appear as a chicken, a vulture, a jackal, a dog, a beggar, or even as a beautiful woman. The unsuspecting victim gets such a shock when a

seemingly ordinary creature turns into a yakku that they cannot resist the onset of the disease.

SAKARABRU

S akarabru is the African god of darkness. He lives in the fetish house that is found at the entrance of every village. This is where all the spirits and gods who control the weather and other important matters live.

Sakarabru has two sides to his personality: sometimes he prowls through the village and gobbles up anyone who is out after dark; at other times he guards the village against attack by evil demons.

FETISHES

A fetish is an object in which a spirit lives. This may be anything from a simple wooden or bamboo box, a skull, an elaborately carved statue, or a pouch made from the skin of a magically powerful creature, such as a cat, a frog or a big lizard.

The fetish is prepared by a sorcerer or medicine man. He leaves a hole for the spirit to enter, and lures it in with incantations or by pouring fresh blood inside the container. The hole is then quickly plugged to keep the spirit inside.

Most fetishes are kept for self-protection. They protect their owners against disease, theft, and attack by wild animals or enemies. The spirit that lives inside the fetish may be an ancestor of the owner, or an alien spirit caught by the medicine man in the forest.

A fetish may sometimes be used for evil purposes. In this case the spirit inside the fetish has to be fed with human blood in order to stay alert and active. The more evil the owner wants his fetish to carry out, the more human flesh it devours.

Motikatika

A long time ago, a man lived with his wife and baby in a little mud hut in an African village. They were all happy together until the wife became ill and refused to get up or to eat. Her husband tried to tempt her with all kinds of delicacies, but she wouldn't take any of them and eventually she became so thin and weak that he feared she would die.

'Is there nothing that you would like to eat?' he asked in despair.

'The only thing I want is some wild honey,' the wife replied.

The husband rushed off to the forest and found a bees' nest at the top of a tree. He climbed up and carefully extracted a piece of honeycomb, which he took back to his wife.

'I can't eat that,' she said in disgust. 'It's got dead bees in it!'

So the husband went out and found another nest, and brought the honeycomb back to his wife as before. This time she said there were ants in it, and the third lot was full of dirt. The fourth bowl of honeycomb was declared fit to eat, and after a few days the wife was strong and well again.

But now the husband decided it was his turn to stay in bed.

'Now you can look after me,' he said. 'I am thirsty and want some sweet spring water.'

The wife took a large jug, filled it at the nearest spring and carried it back on her head.

'I can't drink that,' said the husband in disgust. 'It's got dead flies in it.'

So the wife went out and found another spring, and brought the water back to her husband as before. This time he said the water tasted of frogs, and the third jugful tasted of water-lilies. The wife set out for a fourth time, travelling a long way before she found a lake where the water was clear and pure. As she bent down to fill her jug a horrible monster raised its head above the surface.

'How dare you steal my water,' the monster growled.

The woman shrank back in alarm. 'Please do not harm me,' she begged. 'You can have my baby, if you will let me go.'

'How will I know which is your baby?' asked the monster.

'His name is Motikatika. I will shave his head and hang some beads round his neck, so that when you come to the village you will know him.'

The monster agreed to this and allowed the woman to go home unharmed. Next day, before she went to the fields to work, she shaved her baby's head and hung some beads round his neck.

However Motikatika had supernatural powers and knew what his mother had arranged with the monster. He consulted his magic bones, and then quickly called together all the babies in the village, shaved their heads and hung beads round their necks.

'If you hear anyone call for Motikatika, you must all answer together,' he told them.

Before long the ground began to shake and the monster came thundering along shouting, 'Motikatika! Motikatika! Where are you?'

'Here I am!' cried all the babies together.

'But I only want Motikatika,' said the monster, looking from one to another in bewilderment. He dared not eat the wrong child, or he might find himself in serious trouble. By the time the woman came back from the fields, he was very hungry and exceedingly cross.

'I will call him myself,' said the woman. 'Motikatika! Motikatika, come here at once!'

Motikatika consulted his magic bones again, and turned himself into a mouse. The monster got tired of waiting for his supper and told the woman he would be back again tomorrow.

'Tomorrow I will send Motikatika out into the fields to pick beans for me,' she said, 'and you can eat him then.'

Next morning Motikatika set out with a basket to pick beans. On the way to the fields he asked the magic bones how to escape from the monster for a third time.

'Change yourself into a bird and snap off the beans,' the bones suggested, 'and the monster will chase you away.' That was what happened.

The monster returned angrily to the hut. 'I will not be deceived any more,' he roared. 'Find me Motikatika or I will eat you instead!'

The woman begged the monster for one more chance. 'Return here this evening,' she said, 'and you will find him in bed under a white blanket.'

Again Motikatika consulted his magic bones, and they advised him to change his white blanket for the red one on his father's bed. That night the monster came, seized the person sleeping under the white blanket and ate him.

When the woman realized what had happened she wept bitterly. But Motikatika said, 'It is only fair that my father should be eaten instead of me. After all, it was he who sent you for the water.'

KILYAKAI

The Kyaka people of the forests in western Papua New Guinea have stories about several types of demons. The kilyakai are the demons of nature – of plants and animals. They are small and ugly, and very malicious. They shoot people with their poisonous arrows and this causes their victims to fall ill with malaria.

The kilyakai steal babies if their mothers leave them unattended for a moment, and in their place they leave their own changelings, horrible looking dwarfs who will grow into savage monsters. They also steal pigs and maltreat them.

BOTTLE IMP

In Malaysia there is a tiny spirit called a polong that is no bigger than a child's finger. The polong is also known as a bottle imp. It is made by a sorcerer in a round-bellied bottle with a narrow neck. The sorcerer puts some blood from a murdered man into the bottle and mutters secret incantations over it. After one or two weeks a pelesit, a cricket-shaped spirit associated with the bottle imp, begins to stir and chirp.

The polong has to be fed on blood. So the sorcerer sends it to an intended victim at night. The cricket enters the victim's body tail first, and the bottle imp follows, to suck the blood. When the victim falls ill, the medicine man is fetched and he asks the polong inside the patient, 'Who is your master?' The cricket answers through the patient's mouth, giving the sorcerer's name in a high-pitched chirping. Once the name is known, the medicine man can extract the spirits.

MOPADITI

The mopaditis are the spirits of the dead who haunt northern Australia. An Aboriginal travelling alone through the bush may sense the presence of a lonely mopaditi. The spirit doesn't like to be alone and will try and steal one from a living

▷▷ One particular bottle imp is supposed to be able to grant its owner anything that he or she might desire. However, there is one catch – if you died still owning the bottle, your soul would go straight to Hell. The only way to get rid of it was to sell it for less than you paid for it. It was last heard of in Tahiti sometime during the 1880s.

person to keep him company. It is sometimes possible to scare off a mopaditi by singing or shouting, but the best thing is to carry a lighted torch and wave it around your head.

YOWIE

When livestock is attacked or devoured on the Australian ranches the local people usually blame the dingoes. However, the culprit might well be a yowie. It is rumoured that these monsters live in deep caves in the Australian outback, coming out at night to steal cattle and sheep.

Those who have seen a yowie say that it looks something like a large insect, although its head is more like that of a lizard. It has six legs like an insect, scales all over its body rather like a beetle or a reptile, and a snake-liketail.

The Bunyip

Bunyips are Australian water monsters. They live in rivers, billabongs and mangrove swamps and come out after periods of rain to eat people. During times of drought bunyips hibernate by burying themselves deep in the mud. This story tells what happened to a foolish young man who tried to steal a bunyip cub from its mother.

One day a group of young Aboriginal warriors set out into the bush in search of food. They were full of high spirits, and as they went along they raced each other, hurling their spears to see whose would go the furthest. Eventually they reached a marshy area where there were several pools surrounded by bulrushes. The roots of these plants are very good to eat.

One of the young men suggested that they collect some roots to take back to their families. But another one said, 'Why waste our time doing women's work. They can come and gather the roots themselves. Let us fish for eels instead.'

This suggestion met with general approval, and they all made themselves fishing rods and searched for worms to use as bait. One of them had a piece of raw meat in his bag that he intended to cook for dinner, so he cut off a small piece and baited his hook with that.

For a long time no one had a single bite, and they were just about to give up and go home when suddenly the one who had baited his hook with raw meat saw his line disappear under the surface. Something was pulling so hard that it threatened to drag him into the water.

His companions ran to help, and between them managed to land not an eel, or a fish, but a creature with a long broad tail that was a cross between a calf and a seal. The young men looked at each other in horror: what they had caught was a baby bunyip!

The little creature wailed in distress, and from across the pool came an answering call. The bunyip's mother rose up out of her den and came lunging across to the bank, her huge yellow eyes flashing with rage.

'Let it go! Let it go!' shouted the young men.

But the one who had caught the bunyip wanted to take it home to show his girlfriend. He hurled his spear at the mother to keep her at bay and raced off with the baby bunyip slung over his shoulders. The others ran after him, and were startled to hear a low rushing sound behind them.

Looking back, they saw that the pool was slowly rising, and the spot where they had landed the bunyip was completely covered with water. Even as they looked, the water advanced upon them.

Taking to their heels, the young men ran as fast as they could until they came to the high ridge of their home village. Only the tops of the trees remained above the water, and those were fast disappearing. The women and children of the village were clinging to each other in terror as they watched the advancing flood.

The young man grabbed his girlfriend and said, 'Let us climb to the top of the tallest tree where the water cannot reach us.' But as he spoke, he felt something cold touch him, and looking down, he saw that his feet had turned into claws, and that his hands had become the tips of wings.

He cried out in horror, but the noise that came from his throat was the hoarse cawing of a bird.

By now the rising flood had reached the young man's waist, and he found that he was floating on the water. The reflection that he saw on the surface was that of a great black bird. Looking around him, the young man saw that he and his friends had all been changed into swans. When the baby bunyip had been carried home by its mother, the water retreated.

None of the other tribes dare to go near that side of the pool, even today. As for the young men, they never changed back from being swans, though sometimes you can hear them talking and laughing with human voices.

The Oceans

In the days of sailing ships, seamen crossing the oceans faced many dangers. Serpents attacked ships and snatched up prey in their huge jaws. Fire-breathing monsters, giant octopuses and enormous whales struck terror into the hearts of the most fearless men.

Even if a ship escaped such animal horrors, it could be sucked into a huge whirlpool or become helplessly trapped in the clogging weeds of the Sargasso Sea.

What happens to wrecked ships and drowned sailors? Some say that they reappear as ghosts to haunt the oceans. Others believe that they find their way into Davy Jones's Locker right at the bottom of the sea.

The Flying Dutchman

Superstitious sailors believe that on stormy nights in the South Atlantic a phantom ship called *The Flying Dutchman* may be seen beating its way against the wind near the Cape of Good Hope at the tip of South Africa.

The Flying Dutchman has been blamed for shipwrecks, and for driving unfortunate seamen on to dangerous rocks and into shoals. Seeing the phantom ship is always a bad omen.

About four hundred years ago, a Dutch captain called Van der Decken killed his brother in a fight and was sentenced to sail away to the South Seas, never again to return to Holland. Sadly, the captain set sail.

Off the southern tip of Africa his ship ran into a violent storm that ripped

the sails and tore holes in the side of the vessel. As the ship tossed in mountainous seas, the crew begged Van der Decken to shorten sail and run for harbour.

'It is nothing but a gentle breeze,' he scoffed. 'Turn the ship into the gale and put your trust in the Devil!'

The crew were all religious men and thought the captain must be mad to mock God in this way. One man seized the wheel and struggled to turn the ship towards shore, but the captain picked him up and threw him overboard.

As thunder roared and lightning flashed the figure of an old man wearing a long white cloak appeared on the deck. 'You are a cruel man,' said the spirit, 'to take all these men to their doom.'

Enraged, Van der Decken stepped forward and raised his clenched fist at the old man, but his arm fell uselessly to his side.

With his other hand he took the pistol from his belt and fired. But instead of striking the apparition, the bullet pierced his own hand.

'You are cursed, captain,' said the old man. 'You are condemned to sail the oceans of the world forever. And you will sail alone, for no crew will serve under such a master. And wherever you sail, a storm will follow you.'

And so the Dutchman began his long, stormy voyage that will only end when the oceans run dry.

KRAKEN

Norse folklore tells how the kraken is frequently seen off the coast of Norway. It seizes sailors or whole ships with its huge tentacles and drags them down to the deep.

One of the kraken's victims was a Danish sailing ship that had been becalmed in the North Atlantic. The captain wanted to keep the crew busy, so he ordered them to scrape and clean the outside of the hull. Suddenly, without warning, a giant sea monster emerged, wrapped two of its enormous arms around two of

Numerous seamen have tried to harpoon the leviathan, but their weapons simply bounce off his skin, which has overlapping scales like a double coat of armour.

SEA SERPENTS

Sea serpents have been reported in all the oceans of the world. They often attacked sailing ships in search of prey. Sometimes a serpent washed men off the decks and into the sea by surfacing alongside a ship and spouting a jet of water. More often, it simply snatched them with its huge jaws.

the men and dragged them into the sea. A third arm went round another sailor, but he clung desperately to the rigging and his shipmates freed him by hacking off the arm. The bodies of the first two men were never recovered, and the third sailor died that same night.

LEVIATHAN

Whenever this enormous sea dragon swims up to the surface the sea boils. The leviathan breathes fire from his mouth, and smoke comes out of his nostrils.

A report of a sea serpent came from the captain of a British ship sailing in the Pacific Ocean. The ship was in full sail and travelling at about ten knots when suddenly the captain felt a strong sensation as if the ship was trembling. The second mate went aloft to see what was happening and saw an enormous serpent shaking the bowsprit with its mouth.

The monster was at least 100 metres long, and five metres around its body. It had glistening green scales on the top of its body, but was white underneath. Fortunately the only damage to the ship was a broken bowsprit, but serpents were often said to destroy small ships by wrapping their coils around them and crushing the timbers.

◁◁ The Leviathan is mentioned in the Bible in the Book of Leviticus. It is also possible that the Leviathan was the beast that swallowed the Prophet Jonah when he was thrown overboard in a storm.

Moby Dick

Back in the old days, when men hunted whales in small rowing boats, a huge sperm whale could often be seen gliding through the dark blue waters of the South Atlantic. His white skin and many scars were instantly recognizable. The whalers called him the White Whale, or Moby Dick. Many men were injured or eaten by his huge jaws.

Sometime in the 1840s Captain Ahab of Nantucket was sailing in the Sea of Japan when he encountered Moby Dick. He and his crew pursued the huge beast in three small whaling boats, trying to shoot the whale with a harpoon. But Moby Dick attacked and destroyed the boats, and bit off one of Ahab's legs. His crew rescued him and took him home, but when his leg had healed Ahab began to yearn for revenge.

In due course Captain Ahab set out to sea again as master of the whaler *Pequod*. His chief officer was Starbuck, a native of Nantucket. Stubb, the second officer, came from Cape Cod. The third mate was named Flask. These officers commanded the *Pequod*'s boats as headsmen.

Each headsman worked with a harpooner. Starbuck was teamed with a young man called Queequeg who came from an island in the South Seas, where his father was the high chief and his uncle a high priest. This young prince was tattooed all over his face and body with a pattern of squares, and had no hair on his head except for one small knot twisted up on top. The second harpooner was an Indian with long black hair, who spoke no English. The third was a huge black man with rings in his ears. On the first morning Captain Ahab called his crew on deck and nailed a gold doubloon to the mast. 'The first man to sight Moby Dick shall have that doubloon,' he said. 'We will chase the monster round the oceans of the world until he is dead.'

During the first week the men took several whales, and whenever they encountered another ship Ahab asked whether her crew had sighted Moby Dick. The *Pequod* sailed down through the South Atlantic, around the Cape of Good Hope and up into the Indian Ocean. When they reached the Sea of Japan, Ahab told the blacksmith to make a special harpoon, which he baptized in the name of the Devil.

A few days later they met the whaling ship *Rachel*, who had seen Moby Dick only the day before. The captain's twelve-year-old son was missing in one of the boats, and he begged Ahab to search for them. However, Ahab refused to help and turned away to hunt for Moby Dick instead. Next day, the *Delight* reported that they had lost five men to the great White Whale.

Ahab did not sleep. For the next four days, he stayed on deck, looking out for any sign of the great White Whale. On the fifth day it was sighted. Ahab armed himself with the special harpoon and set out in pursuit.

Finally Captain Ahab came within reach of his enemy and tried to sink his harpoon into the great whale's side. But Moby Dick charged and sank the boat. The harpoon line caught Ahab and dragged him under. Only one of the *Pequod*'s crew survived to tell the tale.

JONAH

W hen a ship runs into a series of storms, or crew are killed, or if the ship suffers some other misfortune, the sailors may suspect that what they call a 'Jonah' is on board.

The original Jonah was a prophet who was told by God to preach to the people of Nineveh, in Assyria, and to warn them that God would punish them for the wicked way in which they were living. Instead of doing this Jonah embarked on a ship that was sailing to Spain.

During the voyage there was a great storm and the superstitious sailors drew lots to discover which person in the ship was responsible for causing this misfortune. The lot fell to Jonah, and he was thrown overboard. The sea instantly became calm again.

Jonah was swallowed by a whale and remained inside it for three whole days until God answered his prayers for deliverance.

The moral of this story is that you should never take an unlucky person, or Jonah, on board ship.

SARGASSO SEA

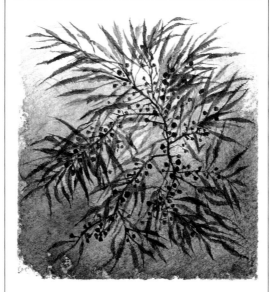

I n times gone by countless sailing ships have been caught in the clogging weeds of the Sargasso Sea. There they drift for weeks on end, unable to move unless the wind blows strongly enough to enable them to break free.

The Sargasso Sea is named after a pale brown seaweed, *Sargassum bacciferum*. This grows along the coasts of North America and is carried on currents across the Atlantic Ocean, to a region southeast of Bermuda. The seaweed has air bladders that keep it afloat, and over the centuries it has accumulated to form a thick carpet on the surface of the sea.

Seamen called this part of the Atlantic the Horse Latitudes because it often happened that they had to slaughter any horses being transported in the ships to provide food. Even so, crews died of thirst and starvation, and their ships' timbers rotted away until they sank to the bottom of the ocean.

DAVY JONES'S LOCKER

When a sailor says that a shipmate or a friend has gone to Davy Jones's Locker, he means that the person named has either been drowned, or has died and been buried at sea.

Davy Jones is the seaman's name for the evil spirit of the sea. He has a huge bosun's locker, or sea chest, where he stows everything that sinks to the bottom. Wrecked ships and dead seamen all find their way into his locker and he never lets them go again.

Many people believe Davy Jones

was once a pirate who committed such a dreadful crime, the Devil condemned him to live forever in the ocean depths.

MAELSTROM

Only very experienced sailors dare to sail between the islands of Mosken and Amoskenaes in the Lofoten Islands off the west coast of Norway. The tide races between the islands, and if there should happen to be an unusually high tide, the wind may turn the waters back on themselves and cause the surface of the sea to spin in a gigantic, foaming whirlpool.

As the whirlpool revolves faster and faster it becomes shaped like a basin. Then the waters turn into a downward-spiralling funnel, reaching down to the seabed.

A whirlpool of this magnitude is called a maelstrom. The word comes from the Dutch *malen*, to grind, and *stroom*, a stream. There are maelstroms in other parts of the ocean, but the one off Norway is by far the most dangerous.

Very few ships have ever survived a maelstrom. Any ship caught in one will be sucked into its vortex and dragged relentlessly down into the ocean depths. The whirling waters grind a ship against rocks and crush its timbers. Wreckage and doomed sailors end up in DAVY JONES'S LOCKER at the bottom of the sea.

U-BOAT GHOSTS

W hen a ship or boat has been wrecked or sunk in particularly violent circumstances, many sailors believe that it reappears as an apparition.

▷ During World War I, the crew of submarine U-17 saw a ghost appear in the bows whenever they surfaced after dark. The ghost was said to be that of a second-in-command who was drowned on a previous voyage when the submarine crash-dived.

Sightings of ghost ships and boats are common in all the oceans of the world. An apparition of a World War II U-boat is frequently seen in the Atlantic. Seamen say it is the ghost of a boat commanded by Captain Klaus Till, who sank a British merchant ship and then shot several of the survivors.

VIKING LONGSHIPS

F or three centuries Viking longships dominated parts of Europe and the Atlantic. The carved dragon's heads on their prows terrified the people of other nations, who thought that they endowed the vessels with the powers of a dragon.

The Vikings raided many lands and robbed, enslaved and killed the

inhabitants. They themselves had no fear of death, and frequently came to a violent end in their own ships. No wonder that people who live near the coast still see visions of ghostly Viking longships looming threateningly out of the mists.

ALBATROSS

A lbatrosses are large birds that roam the oceans of the southern hemisphere. They are covered in very thick feathers, so are able to live in freezing climates. Sometimes they are the only living creatures that

sailors see for several weeks in the Antarctic seas.

These huge birds are protected by the spirits of the air and the sea. A sailor who kills one of them is certain to offend the spirits and bring disaster to his ship. The only way to placate the spirits is to tie the dead bird round the offender's neck and lash him to the mast.

MERMAIDS

People who live near the sea will tell you that there are half-human, half-fish creatures who live in the water, but sometimes appear above the surface. The common name for these beings is mermaids, or mermen if they are male. They are also sometimes called sea-maids and sea-men, and in Greek myths they were known as tritons.

These sea people are dangerous to ordinary mortals. Sailors know that seeing a mermaid often foretells death at sea by drowning. Mermaids also sit on rocks combing their beautiful long hair and singing alluring songs. When sailors come close by in order to see and hear them better, their ships are wrecked on rocks.

Mermaids are well-known for taking ruthless revenge if thwarted or slighted in any way. In one story a mermaid gave a young man the gold, silver and diamonds that she had gathered from a wrecked ship. The youth took the gifts, but gave some of the jewels to his mortal sweetheart. Even worse, he failed to meet the mermaid on a couple of occasions as arranged. The

mermaid was angry and jealous. One day she met the young man in a boat and rowed to a nearby cave, saying that it held all the treasures ever lost in shipwrecks. Once there, the young man fell asleep and woke to find himself tied to a rock by gold chains. And so he was held prisoner at the bottom of the sea for ever more, a victim of his own greed.

There are stories of mermaids marrying humans and remaining on land for many years. It is said that a mermaid has an enchanted cap without which she cannot return to sea. If a man manages to steal her cap and hide it, he can marry her. But if she ever finds it she will immediately vanish into the waves.

Experiments

The urge to experiment and explore the unknown has been and will always be with us. In the Middle Ages people believed in alchemy and the Philosopher's Stone, an elixir which could cure all illnesses and make people live for ever. Learned men like Dr Faustus of Heidelberg longed for infinite knowledge and to have power over everything.

In more recent years monsters have been created in scientific laboratories. The man-made monsters of today are every bit as frightening as dragons and giants were to our ancestors.

JEKYLL AND HYDE

A person who has two very different sides to their character may be called a 'Jekyll and Hyde'.

Dr Jekyll was a good and clever doctor, but he had a bad side to his character that no one knew about, and that he wanted to keep to himself. In his research, Dr Jekyll discovered a drug that enabled him to separate this bad side from the good and make it a real person, whom he called Mr Hyde.

By taking his drug Dr Jekyll was able to turn into Mr Hyde and enjoy being evil without any twinges of conscience. Mr Hyde even looked quite different from the smooth-faced, genial Dr Jekyll. He was a pale, dwarfish man with a malicious smile and a husky, broken voice.

Dr Jekyll dosed himself with the drug at frequent intervals and went out to do wicked deeds as Mr Hyde. Then one night, coming home from a night of debauchery, he met an old friend, Sir Danvers Carew, and took offence at something he said. Without even stopping to think he beat the old man to death with his walking stick.

Dr Jekyll was so shocked by this incident that he vowed never to take the drug again, but then discovered that he changed into Hyde without intending to at all. In the end he couldn't escape from Hyde any more, changed for the last time, and poisoned himself with prussic acid.

FRANKENSTEIN'S MONSTER

Many students have sought to understand the mysteries of creation. One such was Baron Victor von Frankenstein, who reanimated corpses and experimented with their component parts. He wanted to create a being that was bigger, stronger and more beautiful than an ordinary human, but what he actually made was a monster.

Frankenstein's monster was a hideous creature. His limbs were in proportion, but the yellow skin hardly covered the bulging muscles and he had dull watery eyes and a shrivelled face. The Baron was so horrified at its appearance that he ran out of the laboratory in terror. When he plucked up the courage to return he found to his relief that the monster had disappeared. From that night on the inhabitants of Ingoldstad in Transylvania slept uneasily in their beds.

After a few weeks the dreadful news came that Frankenstein's young brother William had been strangled. Although the Baron suspected the monster, the nursemaid was accused of the murder and executed. Some time later the Baron was on the slopes of Mont Blanc when his creation suddenly confronted him. The monster said he was lonely and wanted a mate. He blamed Frankenstein for making him so ugly that everyone rejected him. When he had strangled William, he had only been trying to cuddle him.

Frankenstein could not face the thought of creating another monster and he fled, first to England and then to Ireland with his friend Henri Clerval. But the monster tracked them down and killed Clerval. Then he strangled Frankenstein's wife on their wedding night.

Finally Frankenstein tried to escape by boarding a ship to the Arctic. The ship became trapped in ice, and Frankenstein perished from the cold. The monster mourned over his creator's corpse and then destroyed himself.

DORIAN GRAY

People who have their portraits painted should take great care, for anyone who makes an image of another person can gain power over their spirit. The danger of image-making is illustrated by the story of Dorian Gray.

Dorian was a wealthy Englishman who lived in London in Victorian times. Like many aristocratic young men, he led a rather aimless existence, taking an interest only in beautiful women and the arts. He himself was a wonderfully handsome young man, with clear blue eyes and golden hair. He was so handsome that Basil Hallward, a well-known portrait artist, wanted to paint his picture.

When Dorian saw the finished picture, he tried to destroy it. It was a wonderful portrait, but Dorian resented the fact that he himself would have to grow old and ugly, while his image retained its youth and beauty. However Basil persuaded him to hang the picture in his library.

Soon afterwards Dorian broke off his engagement to Sybil Vane, an actress. He behaved so cruelly towards her that she poisoned herself. When Dorian next went into the library, he saw that cruel lines had appeared around the mouth of the portrait, although his own face remained as unlined and beautiful as ever.

Dorian moved the picture to an upstairs room where no one could see it, and, in the following years, led such a wicked life that people were shocked by the scandals that circulated in London society. However, those who gossiped about his disreputable behaviour were surprised to note that Dorian's face remained as innocent as that of a young boy.

Then one day Basil Hallward came to the house and asked to see the picture again. To his horror Hallward saw the portrait of a hideously ugly, cruel old man. Dorian blamed Hallward for painting a portrait so beautiful that he had wished the image, rather than his own face, would reflect his evil ways. In his anger, Dorian stabbed Hallward to death, and the hands of the portrait immediately became stained with blood.

Dorian continued his wicked ways until he fell in love with an innocent young girl, and decided to reform. Thinking that the portrait would surely reflect his new life, he went to look at it again. But he saw an image that was even more repulsive than before, and the blood on the hands was as bright as ever. He stabbed furiously at the painting with the knife that had killed Basil Hallward, hoping that he could kill the past and start again.

When Dorian's servants finally dared to enter the room, they found a dead man with a knife in his heart. The body was so old and ugly that they only recognized it as their master from the rings that he wore. And above the body of the corpse hung the most wonderful, life-like portrait of Dorian Gray in his youth, smiling and beautiful.

ALCHEMY

Alchemy is the ancient art of changing base metals into gold or silver. In the Middle Ages, alchemists also believed in the Philosopher's Stone, an elixir that could cure all illnesses and make people live for ever.

An old legend tells how, centuries ago, an alchemist was bending over a boiling pot filled with a strange mixture from which he hoped to make gold. When he looked up, he saw the Devil at the window. He rushed out, grabbed the Devil by his tail and pulled it off. When he threw the tail into the magic pot, the mixture turned into gold.

Egyptian priests knew how to get pure gold from the earth. They also knew how to make glass, soap, dyes, stains, drugs and poisons, and could perform many other experiments.

Alchemy was brought to Europe by the Moslems who conquered Spain. An Englishman translated the old Arabic writings that contained all the knowledge of the Egyptian and Greek alchemists.

HOMUNCULUS

From some of their experiments alchemists are said to have made tiny human beings called homunculi.

A German physician and alchemist called Paracelsus was rumoured to be the first person to create an homunculus. He put various ingredients into a glass tube and then incubated it for forty days in a barrel of horse manure. When he opened the tube he found a tiny little man, which he fed with human blood to keep it alive.

▷ Alchemists were terrified of having their secrets stolen by rival alchemists, or by the ruler of the land in which they lived – all rulers are permanently short of ready cash!
In order ro protect their secrets, they used codes and symbols to disguise their ingredients and methods from the casual reader, or the enterprising thief or spy.

Steel, iron or Mars
Gold or Sol
Loadstone
Black sulphur
Soap
Quicksilver or Mercury
Precipitate of Quicksilver
Bath
Lead or Saturne
Ashes
To precipitate
Quick lime
To purify
Earth
Waxe
Urine
Note of Distillation
Sand
Water   Aquafortis   Fire

GOLEM

A different type of animated being was made by Rabbi Low ben Bezalel of Bohemia. He made a clay figure that he called a golem, from the name given to Adam before Jehovah breathed life into him. The golem was made to protect the Jews of Prague against attack by Christians.

The rabbi used pure water and clay from a new pit to make the little figure. As he fashioned each part, he blessed it. The golem was brought to life by inserting a slip of paper with the sacred word *shem* written on it under the clay tongue.

The golem scared away the Christians who prowled around the Jewish quarters, and it also did all the cleaning in the rabbi's house. Each Friday night the rabbi removed the life-giving slip of paper from beneath the golem's tongue, so that like all Jews it would cease to work until sunset on Saturday.

However one Friday night the rabbi forgot to remove the slip of paper and the golem ran riot. In the end it was captured and locked away in the cellars of the Great Synagogue in Prague. According to tradition, it lies there still, waiting to be reanimated.

ANONYMA

The story goes that an even more gruesome experiment was carried out during the last century by a famous physician called Dr Robert Terriman. He tried for many years to bring the dead back to life, and at last decided to make an artificial body controlled by a living brain. He called it Anonyma.

Anonyma's body consisted of a series of cogs, pulleys and wheels encased in a skin made of kid leather. To this Terriman connected a head taken from a corpse. The brain was kept alive with injections of a special fluid, and operated the artificial body through a system of nerves. However the brain was that of a brutal criminal, and the humanoid soon began to misbehave and cause trouble.

The end came when Dr Terriman exhibited Anonyma at a scientific conference. The audience laughed at the humanoid's horrible appearance, and Anonyma was so furious that he turned on his creator and broke his neck. Then he tore off his own head and threw it at the audience.

The Undead

From earliest recorded times people have believed that the dead can return from the grave to visit their loved ones. Certainly someone who has committed an evil crime, or the victim of evil, is said to be fated to return after death as a ghost. Tormented souls forever haunt the world of the living in their search for peace.

Of all the horrors possible, one of the worst is to be buried alive. What happens when the supposed corpse awakens, and tries to claw its way out of the coffin? Could this be the origin of the stories of vampires, the bloodsucking undead?

VAMPIRES

Vampires are corpses, neither dead nor alive, that rise from the grave at night and suck the blood of the living. According to old folktales, vampires can take the form of a wolf, or a bat, or even a misty vapour without shape.

A vampire hypnotizes its victim while it feeds so that the person remembers nothing of the gruesome experience, but simply complains of disturbed sleep and a strange lack of energy. Sometimes there are tell-tale puncture wounds on the victim's neck, but usually the wound is sealed afterwards, leaving no more than a faint red mark.

When the feast of blood is over, the vampire crawls back into its coffin to reappear the following night. As the days pass the victim becomes paler and weaker, until at last they die.

Blood from the living keeps the vampire's corpse from decaying. A vampire's corpse can easily be recognized by the excellent state of preservation of its body. No matter how long a vampire has been buried, it will always look alive. If the coffin of a vampire is opened, the body inside will have bright eyes and colour in its cheeks. The hair and nails will still be growing.

One of the chief reasons for people's acute fear of vampires is their power to infect victims with their own insatiable lust for blood.

According to some traditions, only people who die from loss of blood after repeated vampire attacks will become vampires themselves. Others maintain that one or two attacks is enough, and that any victim of a vampire will come back as a new vampire after their natural death. Poppyseeds should be sprinkled inside the coffin of a person who has died from a vampire kiss, and a branch from a thorn tree placed on the lid.

It is sometimes possible to prevent a vampire entering a bedroom by putting salt round the windows and doors, and keeping a cross under the pillow. Salt, garlic, and crucifixes are traditional vampire repellents.

Someone who has been attacked may try to protect themselves by eating earth from the vampire's grave, or rubbing themselves with the vampire's blood. But the only effective way to destroy a vampire completely is to take the corpse to a new grave, preferably dug at a crossroads, and plunge a stake of elder through its heart.

LILITH

The original vampire was Lilith, Queen of the Night and Mother of Demons, who was Jehovah's first flawed attempt at making a woman. Lilith was created out of mud to be Adam's wife, but her soul was damaged and she gave birth only to evil spirits. She deserted Adam to join Satan's retinue, and Jehovah made a replacement woman called Eve from one of Adam's ribs.

Lilith became jealous of Eve, the Mother of Mankind, and developed a hatred of children. She is said to steal babies at night and carry them off to the desert. Often she appears at the bedside of a woman who is about to give birth, so that she can snatch the new-born infant.

This demoness also preys on young men, who are seduced by her beauty. The only thing that sets her apart from other women is the coarse black hair on her legs. But she keeps her legs covered, so that no man may see them and recognize her for what she is.

A sure protection against her is to write the words, 'Adam and Eve may enter herein, but not Lilith the Queen' on your bedroom door.

SUCCUBI

The evil spirits who were the offspring of Lilith and Adam are called incubi and succubi. The succubi are female, and they visit and seduce men in their dreams.

DRACULA

The true home of vampires is in Eastern Europe. The vampire legend as we know it today grew up in Romania and Hungary at the beginning of the 16th century, whenreports of vampires were numerous.

Count Dracula was a famous vampire who lived in Transylvania, a province of Romania. His real name was Vlad (or Count) Tepes, and he was a descendant of a long line of cruel lords who liked to impale prisoners on pointed stakes and watch them die while they ate their dinner.

Count Dracula was an evil-looking man, with arched nostrils, blood red lips, long sharp teeth and hair in the palm of his hands – all characteristics of vampires.

Dracula lived in Transylvania for about three hundred years, staying alive by drinking the blood of the peasants on his estate. By the 1890s there were not many peasants left, so he decided to buy some property in England.

A young estate agent called Jonathan Harker went to Dracula's castle to negotiate the deal, and during the night a female vampire feasted on his blood. Soon afterwards Dracula went to England and drank the blood of Harker's young wife.

By this time Harker realized what he was up against. He and some friends chased Dracula back to Transylvania and while Harker cut his throat, one of the others impaled him on a stake.

GHOSTS

Those who have suffered a tragedy during their life on earth are often said to come back as ghosts. A person who has been killed in a car crash, a child who has been drowned, or someone who has been murdered, will rise from the grave to haunt the site of their untimely death. Those who have committed evil crimes also come back to the scene of their earthly transgressions.

▷ One of the most famous ghosts was that of one of the kings of Denmark. His spirit appeared to his son, Prince Hamlet, at Elsinore and incited him to take revenge on the king's murderer – his brother Claudius – who had also married Gertrude, Hamlet's mother. Hamlet eventually killed Claudius, but was killed himself by treachery at the same time.

It is believed that a ghost can be laid, or released, if it is allowed to unburden its trouble or story to a sympathetic listener. Otherwise it may be driven out, or exorcized, by using a holy name.

Sometimes, as in the case of the Cold Boy of Hilton, a ghost may be laid by receiving whatever it lacks. The Cold Boy was the ghost of a stable boy who had been killed by one of the past lords of Hilton. In real life, he was always cold, and so the ghost had a disconcerting habit of getting into bed with people to warm himself. He was finally laid by a gift of clothing.

DOPPELGANGER

If anyone has ever accused you of a crime you didn't commit, or seen you in places where you haven't been, then you may have a doppelganger.

The word doppelganger means 'double-goer' or 'co-walker'. Unlike a shadow, which is cast by the sun, a doppelganger is an apparition of a living person. It is invisible to humans, but can be seen by animals, particularly by dogs and cats. If you ever have the feeling that your pet cat is looking past you rather than at you, it is because the cat has seen your doppelganger.

For most people, most of the time, a doppelganger is a pleasant companion. It stands exactly behind its owner and imitates their movements and voice, rather like an echo. However, sometimes a doppelganger decides to act of its own accord, and that is when it gets its owner into trouble.

In some places a doppelganger is believed to be a death token, and may be seen by the doomed person or by a friend.

MANES

These ghosts of the dead live in the centre of the earth. They are shy and harmless, though they have been known to come up through shafts to lead potholers and miners astray.

GHOULS

In Moslem countries a ghoul is said to be an evil spirit, covered with coarse grey hair and with long sharp fingernails, that is supposed to rob graves and prey on human corpses.

One story from Persia tells of how a young man called Noureddin tried to save his dead wife's body from attack by making a bargain with a ghoul. The ghoul agreed to reprieve the body if Noureddin brought him each night for the next eight nights a body that he had killed with his own hands. Horrified at this request, he nevertheless agreed to the bargain.

For seven nights Noureddin went out and killed a passerby. But before he could kill his eighth victim, he was accused and brought before the Cadi. Having heard his story, the Cadi gave judgement. To everyone's surprise, Noureddin was set free to make his own atonement for his crimes.

Next day another half-eaten body was found in the graveyard – Noureddin had killed himself in order to fulfil the judgement of the Cadi and to keep his bargain with the ghoul by providing the required number of corpses.

WINDMILL SPIRITS

According to ancient legends, the weather is controlled by spirits of the air. One group of spirits lives at the top of windmills. They are in charge of the wind that turns the sails. Millers are advised to keep on the right side of these spirits, otherwise they may find that the wind is constantly changing direction and hindering the grinding of their corn.

The Whistling Room

If a house is being haunted by a particularly troublesome spirit, the occupants may ask for the help of someone who is able to 'lay' ghosts. A gentleman called Carnacki was one such expert. The case of the whistling room was one of the most peculiar and horrible cases of haunting that he ever witnessed.

Iastrae Castle in Northern Ireland had recently been bought by an American called Tassoc. An acquaintance of Carnacki asked if he could help Tassoc with what appeared to be a supernatural problem.

When Carnacki arrived at Iastrae, he found the castle occupied only by Tassoc, his young brother Tom and another American called Graves. The three were having to manage for themselves because all the servants had taken fright and left. During dinner that evening Carnacki found out why.

One of the rooms in the east wing of the castle had the most dreadful whistling in it – not an ordinary whistling, but an infernal noise that sounded like an evil spirit trapped in Hell.

'The whistling started the second night we were here,' explained Tassoc. 'Tom and I were in the library at about ten o'clock when we heard this queer whistling coming along the corridor. We took the lamps and went to have a look. As we opened the door of the room, the sound seemed to hit us in the face, and left us stunned and bewildered. We shut the door quickly and got out of there as fast as we could.

'Next day we armed ourselves with guns and had another look at the room and everything was normal. We even hunted all round the grounds and found nothing unusual. I myself am not so sure that it is a haunting. I think it may be someone playing a trick on us.

'You see I am soon tobe married to a local lady

called Miss Donnehue. There are several young Irishmen round here who have been trying to court her for years, so naturally they are somewhat jealous of me.

'On the evening that we celebrated our engagement I told everyone that I had bought this place. I saw smiles on the faces of some of the young men present, and one of them asked whether I wasn't afraid of the whistling room. Apparently several people have bought Iastrae Castle over the last twenty years, but it very quickly comes up for sale again. The chaps bet me that I would not stay here for six months, and I don't intend to lose.'

Just as Tassoc finished speaking, Tom suddenly called out, 'Sssh! Listen!' and Carnacki heard a strange, keening whistle coming from some distance away. All four men ran out of the door, up the stairs and down a long corridor. As they got closer the eerie sound filled the passage, so that the air seemed to throb with some huge evil force. Tassoc unlocked the door and gave it a push with his foot, at the same time drawing his revolver. The others followed him inside.

As Carnacki stepped into the room he was deafened by the shrill,e monstrous whistling. Yet clearly he heard an urgent voice in his ear which seemed to be saying, 'Get out of here! Get out of here quick!' In an instant he pushed the others out into the passage. As he slammed the door behind them there was a hideous yelling scream in the whistling, followed by sudden silence.

That night, after the others had gone to bed, Carnacki hung some protective garlic round his neck and returned to the whistling room alone. The room was still silent, but ominously so, as if it were full of a purposeful, wicked silence. Working as quickly as he could, Carnacki sealed windows and the opening of the fireplace with seven lengths of human hair.

Just as he was finishing his task a low, mocking whistling began to grow in the room and, as he made a dash for the door, the sound reached a horrible crescendo. Carnacki sealed the door with crossed hairs and then went back to the safety of his room.

In the morning Carnacki found the seals on the door and windows intact. But on the fireplace the seventh hair that he had put across the others was broken. It seemed hardly possible that anyone could have entered the room by way of the chimney and passed through the fireplace leaving six hairs intact.

A thorough search of the whole room and then of the whole castle and its grounds revealed no clues. Yet each night the terrible whistling continued – though Carnacki's attempts to record it on a phonograph proved useless.

Carnacki was called away from Iastrae for a few days, and on his return had to walk up to the castle because he had not warned Tassoc of his arrival. As he passed the east wing he heard the same macabre whistling from the room and suddenly he thought that if he fetched a ladder, he could look into the haunted room from the outside.

Peering in through the window Carnacki saw that the centre of the floor was puckered upwards into a strange rubbery mound with a gaping hole in it – a hole that heaved and pulsed to the rhythm of the whistling. Suddenly he realized that what he was looking at were two enormous, repulsive lips. Then he heard Tassoc's voice calling for help from within the room.

Carnacki broke through the window and raced across to the fireplace, from where Tassoc's voice seemed to come – but there was no one there. A frightful, triumphant whistling scream filled the room and the end wall bellied-in towards Carnacki in the shape of two enormous lips. Then there was a sense as of dust falling, continually and monotonously. Sick with fear, Carnacki threw himself across the room and plunged headlong out of the window, crashing on to the ladder and slithering more or less safely down to the soft wet grass of the lawn.

When he had recovered Carnacki went round to the front of the castle and knocked up Tassoc. He told him what had happened and said that, in the morning, the room would have to be destroyed and every fragment of it burned in a furnace erected within a pentacle. During the demolition an old inscription was found above the fireplace which said that Dian Tiansay, the jester of King Alzof who had composed the *Song of Foolishness* about King Ernore of the Seventh Castle, had been killed in the room.

According to an old parchment they found in the library, a long time ago there had been two kings called Alzof and Ernore who were sworn enemies. Nothing more than a little raiding went on until Dian Tiansay made up his *Song of Foolishness* about King Ernore. King Alzof enjoyed it greatly and gave the jester one of his court ladies as a wife. Soon everyone was singing the song, and King Ernore was so angry that he waged war on Alzof and burned his castle.

Dian Tiansay was brought to Iastrae Castle, his tongue was torn out and he was imprisoned in a room in the east wing. The jester's pretty wife Ernore kept for himself. One night she was nowhere to be found, but in the morning she was discovered lying dead in Dian Tiansay's arms. He was whistling the Song of Foolishness because he could no longer sing it. And so Dian Tiansay was roasted in the great fireplace, and thereafter the terrible whistling was heard in that same room as the murdered jester vainly sought his revenge.

△ When Satan rebelled against God, he had many angel followers. They were thrown out of Heaven at the same time and, according to their powers as angels, became different kinds of devils. The least became imps; the great ones like Mephistofeles do deals with foolish humans.

DOCTOR FAUSTUS

D octor Faustus was a learned doctor of the University of Heidelberg in Germany who secretly studied magic and alchemy. He longed to have power over everything and so he promised his soul to a devil named Mephistofeles when he died, on condition that the devil would give him all the magical powers that he craved during his lifetime.

Thus Faustus turned away from God to get knowledge and power for himself. His punishment came when, at the end of his life, the

Devil claimed his soul and bore him off to eternal damnation.

SATAN

T he supreme spirit of all evil is called Satan, a Hebrew word which means 'one who takes the opposite side'. In the Old Testament Satan is often called 'the adversary'. Another name for Satan is the Devil, which comes from a Greek word meaning 'to set one against another'. The Devil's chief object is to break the relationship between God and man.

Satan was once a mighty angel who tried to make himself the equal of God and as a result was cast out of Heaven. His name before his fall was Lucifer. Satan rose from the lake of liquid fire into which he had been thrown and, with the help of the other angels that had fallen with him, plotted and carried out his vengeance on God by tempting Adam and Eve to disobey God. Since then Satan has appeared to all sorts of people, making tempting offers for their souls.

The Devil and the Peasant

The Devil who appears in many European folktales is a very different sort of creature from Satan. He is shown as an evil, but stupid, character who is easily foiled by those he seeks to deceive. The following story tells how one crafty peasant made a fool of the Devil.

A peasant worked hard in his field from dawn until dusk. He was just getting ready to go home one evening, when he noticed a heap of burning coals in the middle of the field. When he went up to it he saw a little black devil sitting on the top of the live coals.

'Are you sitting on a treasure?' asked the crafty peasant.

'Yes indeed,' said the Devil. 'On a treasure that contains more gold and silver than you have ever seen in your life.'

'Well, the treasure lies in my field and therefore it belongs to me,' said the peasant.

'It is yours,' answered the Devil, 'if for two years you will give me one half of everything that your field produces.'

The peasant agreed to the bargain, but said, 'So that there is no dispute about the exact division, everything above ground will belong to you, and everything under the ground will belong to me.'

The Devil was well satisfied with this, but the crafty peasant had sown turnips in the field.

At harvest time, the Devil appeared to take away his crop, but found nothing but yellow, withered leaves. The peasant was busy digging up his lovely big turnips.

'Well, I see you have got the better of me this time,' snarled the Devil. 'Next year what grows above the ground will be yours, and what grows below the ground is mine.'

The peasant agreed, but this time he sowed wheat in his field. At harvest time the peasant went to the field and gathered in the ripe grain. The Devil found nothing left for him but stubble. He was so furious that he stamped his foot and disappeared down a cleft in the rock. And the peasant went and collected the treasure.

✳ Further Reading ✳

There are hundreds of books about monsters, ghosts, ghouls, sorcerers, witches and their doings. Go and look in your local library or your nearest bookshop and you will find a good choice of books to investigate. The following list includes some classic stories that you should look out for and some books for adults which you might find interesting. You should be able to buy most of the children's stories in paperback.

A good collection of myths and legends from around the world can be found in the Oxford University Press's (OUP) series: OXFORD MYTHS & LEGENDS.

If you like horror stories, try the POINT HORROR series published by Hippo and the NIGHTMARE series published by Lion.

Classic children's stories

Aarrgh! The Monster Hunter's Guide, Jim and Duncan Eldridge (Red Fox).

Beowolf, Robert Nye (Orion's Children's Books).

The BFG, Roahl Dahl (Puffin).

A Book of Spooks and Spectres, Ruth Manning-Saunders (Puffin).

Dr Jekyll and Mr Hyde – and other stories, Robert Louis Stevenson (Puffin).

Dracula, Bram Stoker (Puffin).

Earthfasts, William Mayne (Red Fox). This author has written several other children's fantasy stories.

The Face in the Frost, John Bellairs (Puffin).

Frankenstein, Mary Woolstonecraft Shelley (Puffin).

Haunting, The, Margaret Mahy (Magnet). This author has written several other fantasy stories.

Hound of the Baskervilles, The, Sir Arthur Conan Doyle (Hippo).

The House on the Brink, John Gordon (Penguin).

Magic!: the story of Sorcery and Wizardry, Jim Hatfield (Horrible Histories, Watts).

Mr Corbett's Ghost and Other Stories, Leon Garfield Puffin).

The Phantom of the Opera, Gaston Leroux (Puffin).

The Pied Piper of Hamlyn, Robert Browning (Orchard Books).

The Shadow-Cage, and other tales of the supernatural, Philippa Pearce (Puffin).

Small Shadows Creep, Andre Norton (Lion). This author has written several other fantasy stories.

Spook! The Story of Things That Go Bump in the Night, Jim Hatfield (Horrible Histories, Watts).

A Treasury of Giant and Monster Stories, A. Spenceley (illustrator) (Kingfisher).

A Whisper in the Night, Joan Aiken (Red Fox). This author has written several other collections of fantasy stories.

Whispering in the Wind, Alan Marshall (Lion).

Young Oxford Book of Ghost Stories, Dennis Pepper (editor) (OUP).

Adult books you might enjoy

The Book of Horror, H.P. Lovecraft (Robinson Books).

Carnacki, the Ghost-Finder, William Hope Hodgson (Tom Stacey).

Encyclopedia of Myths & Legends, Stuart Gordon (Headline).

Encyclopedia of Things That Never Were, Michael Page and Robert Ingpen (Dragon's World).

The Ghouls, Peter Haining (editor) (Chancellor Press).

The Hound of Death; and other stories, Agatha Christie (Fontana).

The Picture of Dorian Gray, Oscar Wilde (Wordsworth Classics).

✳ Index ✳